The Internationalization of Police Cooperation in Western Europe

SMP - Cahier 6

The Internationalization of Police Cooperation in Western Europe

Cyrille Fijnaut
editor

Gouda Quint bv
Arnhem

Kluwer Law and Taxation Publishers
Deventer • Boston

1993

Kluwer Law and Taxation Publishers
P.O. Box 23
7400 GA Deventer/The Netherlands
Tel.: +31 5700 47261
Fax: +31 5700 22244
Telex: 49295

6 Bigelow Street
Cambridge, MA 02139/USA
Tel.: +1 617 354 0140
Fax: +1 617 354 8595

Gouda Quint
Postbus 1148
6801 MK Arnhem
Tel.: 085-454762
Fax: 085-514509

ISBN: 90 6544 7210

Foreword

Some years ago, the Dutch Police and Society Foundation decided to institute a bi-annual 'Publication Prize'. This prize, which was awarded for the first time on 22 October 1992, went to Dr. W. Bruggeman for his dissertation: '*Naar een vernieuwde statistiek voor de reguliere politiediensten in België*' (Towards More Modern Statistics for the Regular Police Forces of Belgium). The laudatio at the end of this book sets out the reasoning behind the jury's choice of prizewinner.

To mark the award of this prize, the Board of the Foundation organized a symposium on a highly topical theme: the internationalization of police cooperation in Western Europe. In order to clarify the complexities of this important development, a number of contributors were asked to analyze and comment on the subject from a national viewpoint. Contributors, some policy-makers and some specialist researchers, included Prof. Dr. M. Anderson (University of Edinburgh), Dr. R. Rupprecht (German Ministry of Internal Affairs, Bonn), Mr L. de Witte LLB (Principal Private Secretary to the Minister of Internal Affairs, Brussels), Mr J. Peek LLB and Mr Hoefman LLB (resp. Ministry of Justice and Central Investigation Information Service, The Hague) and Prof. Dr. E. Nadelmann (Princeton University). In the general introduction I myself gave an outline of the main aspects of Western European policies with regard to international police cooperation. This compilation, however, not only includes the texts of speeches from the 22nd of October, it also includes a supplementary paper written earlier by Prof.Dr. M. Anderson on the views held in France on international police cooperation in Western Europe and a paper of mine regarding police cooperation across the Dutch-Belgian border, right in the middle of the Benelux, the forerunner of the European Community.

In conclusion, it only remains for me to thank the Director of the Police and Society Foundation, Mr J. van der Steege, and his staff – in particular C. van der Vijver, Mrs G.J.M. Lassche-de Hoon, J.J. Roth and W. Oosterhof – for their indispensable assistance in the organization of both the award ceremony and the symposium, and also in the publication of this book.

Prof.Dr. Cyrille Fijnaut

Contents

The Internationalization of Police Cooperation in Western Europe

Cyrille Fijnaut

I. Introduction

In the coming years international police cooperation in Western Europe will undergo a lot of change, at least when the Treaties which embody its regulation and organization have been ratified by the States concerned: the Schengen Convention and the Maastricht Treaty on European Political Union. This thesis can be easily proved by an analysis of the relevant provisions in these Treaties. But such a demonstration does not take away that the political unanimity these provisions at first sight radiate, is to some extent very misleading: in fact they are the miraculous result of laborious negotiations between senior representatives of the Member States of the European Community or, to put it simply: they represent complicated political compromises.

If only to gain an adequate understanding of the named Treaties in the field of police cooperation it is necessary to explain the philosophies the Parties to these Treaties in general honour with respect to this issue and, in particular, the standpoints that they have defended in 'Schengen' and in 'Maastricht'. However, this is not the only reason why the Dutch Police Foundation has asked some of the important architects and observers of the restructuring of international police cooperation in Western Europe, to explicate today the perspectives and arguments which play a vital role in the policy their respective governments support with a view to international policing in this part of the European, the Western world. The other, the second reason returns to the idea that a profound insight into the similarities and differences between the States concerned into this respect is a necessary condition for any appraisal of the future evolution of international police cooperation. To what extent are they really willing to invest money, time, people into the application of the agreements made in the Schengen Convention and the Maastricht Treaty? And – in the long term – which outlooks for yet more radical changes are realistic or completely untenable? I hope that Prof. dr. M. Anderson, dr. R. Rupprecht, mr. L. de Witte and Mrs M. Hoefman – in close cooperation with mr. J. Peek – will be able to give us an idea of the answers to these questions.

All this, however, does not justify the presence of Prof. dr. E. Nadelmann in our midst. Nevertheless his contribution to this conference is also very important. Not only because transatlantic police cooperation – via Interpol as well as via the liaison officers of the FBI (Federal Bureau of Investigation) and the DEA (Drugs Enforcement Administration) at our American embassies – has become a frequent affair, but also because the DEA in particular considers Western Europe as an important part of its global battle field. In other words: reorganization of international police cooperation in Western Europe in one way or another implies a restructuring of the working relationship with the federal American police services. Therefore I hope that Prof. E. Nadelmann will inform us about the foreign police policy of the American government in relation to Western Europe. For the rest I want to make the observation that insight in the federal police system of the United States is also a prerequisite for any estimation of the prospects for international police cooperation in the difficult process of economical and political unification of Western Europe.

My own contribution to this conference is mainly intended to provide some of the background knowledge one should have in order to understand the contributions of the other speakers. Above all this means that I shall present a more or less reflexive and critical overview of the complicated structures of international police cooperation which presently exist in Western Europe.

II. The Unstable Position of Interpol

Of old, at least from 1923, Interpol has been the most important cooperation mechanism in Europe and, in any case since World War II, over the whole world. Today the 2 main functions of Interpol are still the exchange of police information, in very diverging forms, and the collection and analysis of data concerning all sorts of international (organized) crime. To strengthen the position of Interpol in the presence of new and more powerful forms of police cooperation in Western Europe a European Secretariat was established in 1986. This Secretariat has to assist the Technical Committee on Cooperation in Europe and the European Regional Conference. Furthermore it ensures liaison between 'Europe' and the other Interpol-regions, it organizes working meetings enabling investigators from different European countries working on the same case to cooperate more closely, and it tries to cover the day-to-day management of complex cases requiring international police cooperation at operational level.[1]

In spite of all this Interpol is not based on an international treaty. This shows that Interpol still functions more or less as an international police association, although its structures are much more formalized than those of the German Polizeiverein in the 19th century. However, it would be completely false to deduce from the fraternal appearance of Interpol that it is a private, non-profit making organization. For a number of reasons it is more appropriate to characterize Interpol as an international public institution sui generis. This judgement is not only founded on its aims and tasks as described in the Constitution of 1956, but also on the role Interpol has been assigned in several treaties relating to legal assistance in criminal matters, on the agreements with the French government concerning such things as the immunity of its personnel and the control of the information stored, and on the fact that states which are involved in the activities of Interpol, at least in theory, pay allowances, send delegates to its meetings, etc.[2]

The ambiguous position of Interpol has nevertheless always been a source of negative criticism, insinuations and so on. At present the (American) National Association of Chiefs of Police (NACOP) is its most important opponent. Its director G.S. Arenberg in a letter of 11 February, 1992, to the Permanent Ambassador of the United States of America to the United Nations wrote the following[3]:

– The United Nations has utilized and funded Interpol on specific projects to combat the illicit drug trade. Yet, an examination of the facts demonstrates that highly placed Interpol officials who controlled the Interpol network in certain countries have abused their office for their own profit by actively engaging in illicit drug trafficking;
– NACOP is also concerned because, despite these activities, and despite Interpol's past as an arm of the Nazis during the Second World War, Interpol operates above the law. Interpol is immune from legal actions around the world. No international oversight mechanism exists over Interpol and Interpol is accountable to no one;

1. ICPO – Interpol General Secretariat, 'The European Secretariat', *International Criminal Police Review, 1990*, no. 424, 10-12.
2. Anderson, M., *Policing the World; Interpol and the Politics of International Police Cooperation*, Oxford: Oxford University Press, 1989, 57-73; Möllemann, H., *Internationale Polizei – Polizei des Völkerrechts*, Würzburg: s.n., 1969.
3. This letter was 'published' on the writing paper of the National Association of Chiefs of Police.

– Although the Interpol Constitution requires members to abide by the Universal Declaration of Human Rights and to refrain from intervening in political, military and religious matters, no mechanism exists to enforce compliance with these requirements;
– There is no question among law enforcement professionals that we need an effective international law enforcement program to combat international crime. However, such a program should be established by Convention so that the organization is held accountable for its actions;
– We respectfully request that the United Nations conduct a comprehensive review of its current relationship with Interpol to determine if Interpol has conformed to the principles and guidelines which are imperative to its good relations with the United Nations.

At a recent round table discussion on Interpol in the Belgian Senate Mr. Arenberg firmly repeated his accusation. But what must we think about its content?

On the one hand I would like to argue that it is a very one-sided attack – the functioning of the American DEA outside the United States is equally very questionable –, that its empirical basis shows weak points – his remark on Interpol during the Second World War is to some extent inappropriate – that it completely leaves aside the intimate involvement of the United States in Interpol during the last fifteen years – e.g. in 1984 the head of the U.S. Secret Service (!) was elected president of Interpol – and that his legal judgement about Interpol lacks the much-needed sophistication.

On the other hand, however, he hits the nail on the head: the position of Interpol is very ambiguous. It is very unclear who its members are: the States or the police chiefs concerned? More importantly, unlike other international, intergovernmental (public) institutions, not only is Interpol not embedded in global, or at least international political structures like the United Nations, the Council of Europe, let alone the European Community, but also has – e.g. at the level of senior officials – no representative structure, emanating from the States concerned, that governs the management and operations of Interpol.

III. TREVI: The First Intergovernmental Counterpart of INTERPOL

It is precisely the 'a-political' character of Interpol that was one of the important factors in the process that ultimately led to the foundation of TREVI in 1975. Interpol, indeed, was not an appropriate mechanism at all to cope with the problem many Member States of the European Community were confronted with at the beginning of the 1970s: terrorist activities of groups and movements of European, but also of non-European origins. Interpol was not a suitable vehicle for the police to tackle this international problem for two reasons. The first one has to do with the prohibition in the Interpol Constitution (Art. 3) that it may not become involved in political, military, religious and racial matters. The second reason is related to the ambiguous legal position of Interpol: the grip of the states concerned on this institution is not strong enough to enable them to use it as their own instrument to steer international police cooperation in such a sensitive matter as (the fight against) terrorism. In short, at the time, in 1975-1976, the political leaders of the European Community had to look for a different solution than the mobilization of Interpol. In doing so they hit upon the idea of creating a radically new, but yet more secretive consultation and cooperation mechanism: TREVI.[4]

The hierarchical structure of TREVI makes clear its real intergovernmental character and, in this way, also its main institutional differences with Interpol. At the top of TREVI are the Ministers of Interior and Justice concerned; they meet twice a year under the chairmanship of the Minister of the Member State that chairs the European Council. At the second level are the Committee of Senior Officials who prepare the meetings of the Ministers and direct the working parties at the third level. The actual four regular working parties are on terrorism (I), on equipment, public order, training etc. (II), on drugs and serious (international, organized) crime (III) and on '1992'. Whereas these topics clearly show that TREVI in some respects doubles the operational tasks of Interpol and so is a challenging rival for it, the structure of TREVI marks in a significant way its institutional difference with Interpol: TREVI really represents an international governmental institution, Interpol only forms a peculiar international police organization. This justifies the conclusion that simply by the foundation of TREVI in 1975 international police cooperation in Western Europe was taken to a level which surpassed anything that has been accomplished or pleaded for the past hundred years in this part of the world.

4. Fijnaut, C., 'The Internationalization of Criminal Investigation in Western Europe', in: Fijnaut, C. and Hermans, R., eds., *Police Cooperation in Europe*, Lochem: J.B. van den Brink, 1987, 32-56.

IV. The Communitization of International Police Cooperation: The Foundation of Europol

However, the debate and policy concerning the economic and, later on, the monetary and political unification of Western Europe have again caused something like an earthquake in this field: the foundation of Europol. One has to give the Germans credit for pushing the debate in Europe for the past twenty years with respect to such a new police institution, or at least such a new police cooperation mechanism. The German literature nevertheless clearly shows that the opinions of the leading figures have always been divided on the way a reorganization of police cooperation in Western Europe should be put into effect. Their ideas not only differed on the role of Interpol in any new arrangement but also on the role of the European Communities and, particularly, the role of the European Commission in this context. But the Schengen Treaty of 1985 already made clear in which direction the knot would be cut. In its annexes the proposal is made that with a view to the fight against the illegal trade in drugs in the long term a central service will be indicated for the exchange of information. In other words: already in this Treaty Interpol (and TREVI) was passed by completely.

It is not necessary to examine now the debates which, over the past years, have taken place in the European Council, the European Commission and the European Parliament with respect to the organization and reorganization of police cooperation at the level of the European Communities. In summary it can be stated that they really prepared the battlefield for Europol. This can, for the rest, also be deduced from the fact that in the Action Programme that was accepted in Dublin in 1990 by the TREVI Ministers and by the European Council, the foundation of a service, as was already mentioned in the annexes of the Schengen Treaty, was programmed for the 12 Member States of the European Community: the European Drugs Intelligence Unit (EDIU).[5] The progression from this project to the declaration in the Maastricht Treaty on Political Union with respect to Europol is not that great: at the TREVI Ministers meeting on 18 September of this year it was decided that the ad hoc group, that has to establish Europol, should redouble its efforts to ensure that Europol is put in place quickly and in particular should see

5. Fijnaut, C., 'Naar een "Gemeenschappelijke" regeling van de politiële samenwerking en de justitiële rechtshulp', in: Fijnaut, C., Stuyck, J. and Wytinck, P., eds., *Schengen: Proeftuin voor de Europese Gemeenschap?*, Arnhem-Antwerpen, Gouda Quint – Kluwer Rechtswetenschappen, 1992, 89-117.

that the first phase, the Europol Drugs Unit, is in place by January 1993.[6]

The original German suggestion aimed at the foundation of Europol in 2 phases: to begin with Europol should only be a centre for the exchange of information and experience, later on it should get original powers to operate (independently?) within the Member States of the European Community. It was predictable that the (other) Member States would radically resist the latter part of this proposal. It was equally obvious that the governments involved would place Europol within the framework of the intergovernmental cooperation. The relevant provisions in the Maastricht Treaty are indeed part of the so-called 'third pillar' in this Treaty: intergovernmental cooperation in the fields of justice and home affairs. Art. K.1, 9 of the Treaty on European Union only concerns 'police cooperation for the purposes of prevention and combatting terrorism, unlawful drug trafficking and other serious forms of international crime (...) in connection with the organization of a Union-wide system for exchanging information within a European Police Office (Europol)'. The annexed Declaration on Police Cooperation only adds that Europol may fulfil the following functions: support for national criminal investigation and security authorities, creation of data bases, central analysis and assessment of information, collection and analysis of national prevention programmes, measures relating to further training, research, forensic matters and criminal records departments.

All this doesn't alter the fact, however, that on the basis of the general provisions in the chapter concerned not only the European Council but also the European Commission and the European Parliament will be involved in the decision-making process concerning Europol. In other words: the Maastricht Treaty effectuates a certain Communitization of police cooperation between the Member States of the European Community. Indeed, apart from the provisions concerning the right of initiative (only for the Member States) and the Committee of Senior Officials (of the Member States), Art. K.4 clearly states that the Commission will be totally involved in all the activities with respect to the field of 'Justice and Home Affairs'. Art. K.6 regulates the participation of the European Parliament: the Chairmanship and the Commission have the duty to inform it regularly about the activities, the Chairmanship is obliged to consult the Parliament on the most important aspects of the cooperation concerned, and the Parliament disposes of the right to ask questions to the European Council and to make recommendations to it. For the rest

6. See the *Press Release* of 18 September 1992 concerning the *Interior and Justice Ministers Meeting* in Brussels.

the institutional position of Europol will be clarified in a specific convention as was decided at the Lisbon Summit. So we have to wait some time for more details concerning this crucial issue. Nevertheless the foregoing shows that the institutional knot has in principle been cut: police cooperation in Western Europe will become more and more an affair of the European Community.

In relation to the existing institutional arrangements the importance of this decision must not be undervalued. Interpol and TREVI are still permeated by the informal and confidential character that always has typified police cooperation in Western Europe. The organization, mission and duties of both institutions are not based on unambiguous international treaties and their operations are still concealed from the general public, let alone the subject of anything like independent, external, democratic review, control or accountability with respect to their work. What is more, both institutions only represent forms of intergovernmental cooperation, although exactly on this point the position of Interpol is very different from the position of TREVI. Whereas Interpol still functions more or less as a fraternal international police association, TREVI forms a real intergovernmental cooperation mechanism between the Member States of the European Community, but completely extraneous to its established institutions like the European Commission and the European Parliament.

V. Conclusion

The position and definition of Europol entail that in the long run this new police institution will take over the task of Interpol, at least within the Member States of the European Community. The fact that the European Drugs Intelligence Unit is renamed the Europol Drugs Unit and that this Unit is not lodged in Interpol, clearly marks the beginning of this development. If the Community becomes more federalized the end-result will perhaps be that Interpol will have the same position in the European Community as in the United States: one of the outside contact points with the police in other continents. At that stage Interpol would really be the complement of Europol.

Being embodied, in the Maastricht Treaty, within the framework of intergovernmental cooperation between the Member States of the European Community, it is obvious that the governments involved have to arrange, in one way or another, the governance of Europol. The most natural solution would be that this important function would be entrusted to TREVI, or at least to a representative body composed of the

TREVI Ministers. The containment of organized crime is after all one of the main aims of this intergovernmental cooperation mechanism. If this should happen, it would mean that in the long run TREVI and Europol would probably fuse together and form one and the same police institution. Parallel to the reordering of the relationship between Interpol and Europol such a development would also considerably reduce the confusing complexity of international policing in Western Europe.

The British Perspective on the Internationalization of Police Cooperation in Western Europe

Malcolm Anderson

I. Introduction

The Maastricht Treaty on Political Union, signed in December 1991 and, in the same month, key decisions taken in Rome setting up the Schengen arrangements created a momentum for improved European police cooperation.[1] In September 1992 the setting up of a Europol project team in Strasbourg and later the same month the announcement by a TREVI Ministerial meeting of a European Anti-Mafia Group attempted to give practical effect to the broad undertakings in the judicial and home affairs chapter in the Maastricht Treaty.[2] These initiatives took place in a complex European political, social and economic environment and it would be a mistake to say that there is *one* British perspective on them. There are a number of British views; although there is an official government view which has been reasonably consistent, it is expressed in very general terms, obscuring the differences within British official and law enforcement circles. This paper presents a British perspective but it is neither the official view of the United Kingdom (UK) nor a British police view – it is the assessment of an observer.

Three preliminary points should be made – these concern the values of the author, the interaction of levels of policy, and assumptions about the effects of '1992' and the Maastricht Treaty.

First, the scholar participating in a debate about adapting to complex change is engaged in political activity. Value judgments are involved

1. The literature on European police cooperation is still sparse. A pioneering and valuable contribution is Fijnaut, C., Hermans, R., eds., *Police Cooperation in Europe,* Lochem: J.B. van den Brink, 1987; see also Benyon, J., Davies, P., Willis, P., *Police Cooperation in Europe; a Preliminary Report,* Leicester Centre for the Study of Public Order, University of Leicester, 1990 and the working papers produced by the Project Team on European Police Cooperation in the University of Edinburgh – the most relevant to this paper is Walker, N., *The United Kingdom Police and European Cooperation,* Working Paper 3, 1991; at a more popular level Clutterbuck, R., *Terrorism, Drugs and Crime in Europe after 1992,* London: Routledge, 1990.
2. *Financial Times,* 18 September 1992.

and these inevitably affect the conclusions of academic analysis. This paper rests on the belief that the movement towards European union is highly desirable and although not, in a strict sense, inevitable, it can only be resisted at great cost to the Member States of the European Community (EC). Closer police cooperation and eventually the development of EC executive police powers are part of this movement.

Second, those responsible for developing policies of police cooperation have to be sensitive to pressures and developments at three levels other than the European – the global, the national and the local. European governments are aware that the most ambitious and most profitable criminal conspiracies are global in character, crossing the boundaries between the developed and less developed worlds.

At the global level, a development with implications for criminal policing, are the regular meetings of heads of government in the G7 which has set up a task force, based in the OECD, on money laundering; this has revealed the immense scale of the problem and national governments have responded to it.[3] The 1988 UN Drugs Convention is the most ambitious global attempt yet undertaken to oblige signatory states to undertake law enforcement measures. This kind of harmonization through international treaty obligations and through harmonization of legal procedures is a basic requirement for systematic police cooperation.

Democratically elected ministers must be responsive to domestic pressures and concern over the incidence of crime. Crime with trans-frontier implications is increasing but most crime requiring police intervention remains highly localized in character – domestic violence, assaults, murder, theft, vandalism and juvenile delinquency. Control and repression require the intervention of social welfare agencies as well as the police and these are organized and coordinated within the states in a variety of ways. Demands from the public, articulated through elected representatives, as well as the immediate and continuing nature of the problems posed, require that governments give these precedence over European and international cooperation – although some political elements, notably on the extreme Right, deliberately exaggerate the connection between international factors (immigration) and domestic law enforcement problems.

Third, the new factors in the European situation are the dismantling of systematic controls at the frontiers to introduce the single market and the moves towards closer cooperation in home and judicial affairs in the Maastricht Treaty. These new factors will result in the blurring of the

3. *Financial Task Force on Money Laundering: Report,* Paris: OECD, 1990; *Financial Task Force on Money Laundering, 1990-91,* Paris: OECD, 1991.

existing police boundaries in that there will be new or intensified systems of cooperation between local police forces (in the frontier regions) and between national police agencies which will not inevitably be mediated through new institutions at the European level. Complex networks of police cooperation are likely to characterize the new Europe rather than a centralized and hierarchical system with Europol at its apex. The most significant developments in international police cooperation in the highly developed world seem likely to take place at the European rather than the global level. British reactions to the new scenario are still in process of formation.

II. Police and Policing Are at the Very Heart of the Concept of the Sovereign State – What Does This Mean in the British Case?

The late 20th century is a period of rapid change in ideas about the state and sovereignty in Western Europe, on a scale which, in retrospect, may be even more radical than the attack on the basis of political legitimacy during the American and French Revolutions at the end of the 18th century. Although this is well understood in many British milieux, there is a reluctance to accept it among sections of public opinion, in elements of the Conservative Party and in traditionalist circles, including influential groups involved in the legal system and law enforcement. There are relatively few points of social and cultural contact between most of the UK population and the non-English-speaking world and this makes British public opinion slow to change.

The concept of sovereignty, deeply engrained in the political habits and culture of Europe, emerged from the writings of thinkers such as Machiavelli, Bodin and Hobbes, and from the political practices of 15th to 18th century when power was more and more concentrated in the hands of the Prince or sovereign. The basic elements of the concept were that a supreme and exclusive source of law was essential to a state, that the sovereign must have the means to enforce the law and that if those means were lacking then the claim to sovereignty was null and void. In the words of Gianfranco Poggi, the state was 'the sole, exclusive fount of all powers and prerogatives of rule.'[4] Some internal force of order, which eventually became the professional police service, was necessary to enforce the law and maintain sovereign authority threat-

4. Oggi, G., *The Development of the Modern State*, Stanford: Stanford University Press, 1978, 92.

ened by criminality, disorder and subversion. The state became, at least in principle, the only guarantor of the physical security of inhabitants of the territory which it controlled.

All countries developed professional police forces in order to maintain internal security but at different times and with differing forms of organization and control. There is an old assumption in the English constitutional tradition, expressed in such 19th century textbooks as A.V. Dicey, *Law of the Constitution,* that police powers, police organization and the criminal justice system were quite different in Britain from those of continental Europe. In this tradition, there were essentially misleading beliefs that the office of constable deriving from the common law, absence of direct government control of the police except in the special circumstances of London and Ireland, the ways of assuring judicial independence, and the sovereignty of parliament were uniquely capable of defending liberties. These beliefs, and the complacency with which they were held, have been eroded but belief in English exceptionalism still influences attitudes towards European cooperation.

Sovereignty also seems to many in the English constitutional tradition to be an indispensable legal concept. It has been commonly supposed that there must be one supreme source of law not subject to higher legislative authority and there must be one final arbiter of what the law is. This clarity about the source of law and its interpretation is thought to be one of the admirable achievements of the modern state and a great improvement over the medieval polity where different jurisdictions administered different laws derived from different sources in the same territory. European economic law is a clear departure from traditional assumptions but there has not as yet been a breach in the principle of legal sovereignty in criminal law.

In executive law enforcement it is only in very exceptional circumstances that a state allows the nationals of another country (even as recruits to its own police forces) to exercise police powers on its territory. Exceptions include the right of hot pursuit in the Schengen Agreement and US direct assistance to the civil power in anti-drug trafficking operations in Latin America. But no international or European authority yet has police powers in criminal matters. Moreover 'policing one's own patch' without interference from the outside has been seen as desirable for practical operational reasons; when police territories have not been clearly defined this has often led to conflict and difficulty.

The doctrine of sovereignty and the felt need to defend a social and cultural identity complement one another. The fairly clear notion of legal sovereignty often becomes associated with the cloudy notion of political sovereignty (which may be loosely defined as political independence). When used by a politician, such as Mrs Thatcher in her Bruges speech of November 1988, the mixing together of the two notions can be very attractive to large numbers of British people. The same mixture was present in the arguments of the French MP Pierre Mazeaud when he brought a case before the French Constitutional Council (which it rejected) challenging the constitutionality of the Schengen Agreement on the grounds it infringed national sovereignty.[5] However, the notion of political sovereignty is a hollow idea in contemporary Europe. In the 1990s the maximum aspiration possible for governments of European states is a greater or lesser degree of autonomy in some areas. Policing is no different in this respect from other areas of government action.

The erosion of the doctrine of sovereignty has been a long and slow process. One dimension of this process was the growth, from the end of the First World War, of permanent international organizations, including the International Criminal Police Commission established in 1923. These organizations gradually accustomed governmental and public opinion in the United Kingdom to regular, institutionalized forms of cooperation. But British opinion accepted late (and some would say only partially) the radically new factor, which in the long term is likely to transform the forms of policing – the widening scope of economic, legal and political integration through the European Communities. This means that the United Kingdom official position almost always favours inter-governmental cooperation rather than the pooling of sovereignty which is the essence of the EC process. In the area of judicial and police cooperation this is clearly evident and likely to remain the case until circumstances compel a change of attitude.

III. The Practical Problems of Crime Control Have Changed in Certain Highly Publicized Areas

Faced by crime control problems, pessimism is sometimes expressed by senior British police officers that general stigma attaching to crime and criminals has declined, but serious crime still has the power to shock large sections of opinion and, therefore, to impel governments to take measures against it. This is particularly the case in the United Kingdom where the 'party of law and order', in power since 1979, has not succeeded in controlling a very rapidly increasing reported crime rate and therefore has actively sought new solutions. As part of this search, there

5. *Le Monde*, 30 June, 27 July 1991.

has been increasing emphasis in British government policy since the late 1980s on taking measures to improve international cooperation in criminal matters. The Drugs Trafficking Offences Act (1986), the Criminal Justice Act (1988), the Extradition Act (1989) and, above all, the Criminal Justice (International Co-operation) Act (1990) as well as the ratification (three decades after they were open for signature) of the European Conventions on Extradition and on Mutual Assistance in Criminal Matters provide solid evidence of a change in priorities and attitudes.

United Kingdom opinion shares the broad agreement in the EC Member States on what constitutes serious crime (in Scots law, crimes as opposed to offences) – murder, kidnapping, traffic in human beings, traffic in drugs, large scale theft and fraud. This consensus on serious crime has led to suggestions that some of them might be designated as 'federal crimes' or 'Eurocrimes' with a common definition and common sentences adopted throughout the EC, and which could be dealt with by a court in any EC country in which the criminal was apprehended. Such suggestions have explicitly been rejected by the British Lord Chancellor in a lecture delivered in Luxembourg in January 1992 which he concluded by saying:'... it is not necessary, and in my view it is highly undesirable, to impose rigid, uniform, legal rules in all of the Community states. Not only is it undesirable, but to believe it would succeed is simplistic.'[6]

Opposition to criminal law harmonization does not imply a lack of seriousness about crime with international ramifications or a lack of commitment to European and international cooperation to catch criminals. As a recent English Law Commission report expressed it – modern technologically based crime knows no territorial boundaries and therefore must be combatted by international cooperation.[7] Vastly improved communications and transport facilities have either increased the incidence or shifted the location of crime in ways which are familiar to British as well all other EC law enforcement officials. Examples are many but some have a particularly high profile. Every available form of transport is used to carry drugs from the African, Asian and South American countries of origin to British distributors and users; the international banking and financial system of the City of London, with its instantaneous electronic transfer of funds, has been used to assist the

6. The Rt Hon Lord Mackay of Clashfern, *Diversity in Unity; European Laws,* Luxembourg: Churchill Memorial Lecture, 1992.
7. Law Commission, *Criminal Law; Jurisdiction over Offences of Fraud and Dishonesty with a Foreign Element,* 1989, Report No. 180, H.C. 318.

laundering of the profits of trafficking. Every large scale serious fraud case in recent years such as the celebrated Guinness and Barlow Clowes cases have involved foreign jurisdictions and, in some cases, first come to light because of evidence uncovered in foreign jurisdictions. The movement of football supporters and rowdy holiday makers has been made possible by the existence of cheap mass transportation systems. The offences associated with this phenomenon are often petty but they can escalate into major incidents as at the Heysel stadium in 1985 where 38 people lost their lives as a result of violent behaviour by English fans; these incidents, it is admitted in the UK, can provoke xenophobic reactions which damage the reputation of the country and the cause of European cooperation.

There has been increased official and public pressure to find solutions to these and other problems, and a broad acceptance in the UK of the view that the boundaries of the state no longer coincide with the boundary of the problems. The official British position is to insist that appropriate boundaries do not tidily correspond with the external frontier of the European Community. Sometimes they are larger, as in the case of cocaine and heroin trafficking, sometimes they are smaller as in many cases of football hooliganism; problems often require intensive bilateral cooperation although a multilateral framework may help bilateral cooperation. A flexible and 'variable geometry' of cooperation is seen by the British government and by British police officers as both desirable and inevitable.

As a recent British parliamentary report on *Practical Police Cooperation in the European Community* emphasized, virtually all forms of crime and all kinds of police-public relations now have transfrontier implications.[8] In a variety of ways, such as giving the National Criminal Intelligence System specific responsibility for international cooperation, and through specialized training programmes, the British police are making progress to adapt to this changing environment. Courses for senior police officers at Bramshill Police College include modules on European policing and officers on them make study visits to European capital cities. Police forces most directly involved in European cooperation such as the Kent police force lay special emphasis on language training and its European liaison unit has a remit to keep the whole force informed of European developments. There have been no lack of initiatives within the police establishment although there may be an ebbing of interest in European cooperation unless Europol quickly establishes a role.

8. Home Affairs Committee, *Practical Police Co-operation in the European Community*, London: HMSO, 1990, 7th Report, 2 vols + Memoranda of Evidence.

IV. The Existence of the European Community Provides Greatly Enhanced Opportunities for Contact Between Law Enforcement Officials

One profound long-term impact of membership of the European Community is its effect on the outlook and behaviour of public servants. Until the development of institutionalized forms of international economic cooperation in the aftermath of the Second World War, Foreign Office officials were the almost exclusive form of official contact between European states and between these states and international organisations. In the European context officials from the specialized ministries of trade, industry, agriculture, transport, and environment (to list the most important) have been in regular contact with each other and with officials of the European Commission and the Council of Ministers. Under the umbrella, first of European Political Cooperation and TREVI, formalized by the Single European Act of 1985 and by the Maastricht Treaty this cooperation has been extended to Ministries of Justice and of Home Affairs. These regular and official contacts allow unofficial and informal relationships to develop. In other words, telephone calls pass from one European capital to another, meetings over the lunch table take place in which questions are asked about the progress of thinking on this or that policy, or whether data exists on various current issues. In the recent past, up to and including a decade and a half after the Second World War, this would have been regarded, at best, as improper, at worst, as espionnage. The potential impact on the British civil service, which has had a particularly secluded existence, is highly significant.

The police function and the police as a professional group have not been well represented at the European level, partly as a consequence of their isolation from the European Commission and the European Parliament. No organization yet exists to represent the interests and views of the police and this has been regarded as a deficiency by senior British police officers. A European Police Council (later a European police programme) was proposed by chief constable Roger Birch when president of the Association of Chief Police Officers of England and Wales.[9] The British police have a considerable degree of independence from government control and therefore Roger Birch perhaps underestimated the difficulties of this proposal for police officers in other systems. In most

9. Birch R.,'Policing Europe After 1992', Address to the Royal Institute of International Affairs, London 19 April 1989; Bentham, K., 'A European Police Council', in: Anderson, M., and den Boer, M., eds., *European Police Cooperation; Proceedings of a Seminar,* Edinburgh: s.n., 1992, 121-131.

Member Countries, police officers are *fonctionnaires, Beamten* - civil servants - and there is a psychological inhibition, and sometimes legal rules, to be overcome before transfrontier representative associations of police officers, with a genuine input into the making of policy at the European level, could be established. The proposal of Roger Birch was an example of the British police influencing the debate on European cooperation, which they regularly attempt through ACPO and its International Advisory Committee.

British police organization is fairly well adapted to European cooperation. There have been structural reforms which are helpful: the setting up of national services in the form of the Serious Fraud Office by the 1987 Criminal Justice Act and the establishment of the National Criminal Intelligence Service in 1991 (which became operational in January 1992) should assist the coordination of national and international enquiries as well as providing a focus for the international police contacts. At the same time, the maintenance of a decentralized police system – Kenneth Clarke the Home Secretary rejected any move towards a national police force as recently as September 1992[10] – allows a flexibility at the local level and a dispersal of responsibilities. The Kent Constabulary, for example, has the responsibility for policing the Channel Tunnel and through its European Unit has an extensive network of contacts in France and Belgium. There remain political, structural and cultural impediments to optimal coordination with other European forces but a positive lead from the government could attenuate these.[11]

Although the Communities and the inter-governmental cooperation associated with them have played a large role in promoting contact at the official level, there are a number of other fora which bring officials involved in law enforcement together – the UN, particularly the United Nations Drugs Division, the General Assemblies and regional conferences of Interpol, the British Commonwealth – particularly the Legal Directorate of the Commonwealth Secretariat, the Council of Europe – particularly its Committee on Crime Problems and the inter-governmental Pompidou Group on controlling drug abuse, the Conference on the policing of capital cities which brings together senior police officials from Eastern as well as Western Europe, and the arrangements at the local and regional level along all the land frontiers and sea frontiers for regular police contacts. There is sometimes a tendency in the United

10. *Guardian*, 29 September 1992.
11. Walker N., *The United Kingdom and European Police Cooperation*, Edinburgh: University of Edinburgh, 1991, Working Paper 3, discusses these impediments in detail.

Kingdom to stress the importance of these, implicitly and sometimes unconsciously, diminishing the importance of specifically EC forms of co-operation.

V. The Enhanced Sense of European Identity has Significant Implications for Policing

Although regional, religious, ethnic and national identities, as well as feelings of loyalty to political institutions are nebulous and intangible factors in social and political life, they are nevertheless all-pervasive and powerful. Policing policies have to take account of them for broadly two reasons; internally, the esprit de corps and discipline of police forces relates directly to understanding and coming to terms with these identities and loyalties; externally, police officers must understand these factors in order to investigate crimes efficiently and intervene effectively in situations of conflict. Only in deeply divided societies like Belgium or Northern Ireland or in those with a high density of immigrants from outside the Community or in frontier regions where traditions confront one another is there a sensitivity on a daily basis to the importance of these factors but they are nonetheless persistent and general.

Despite trends towards internationalization and Europeanization, the available evidence suggests that national identity and loyalty to the state remain strong in Europe. States and nations are unlikely to be submerged in a wider European identity and loyalty on any time scale which is relevant to contemporary policing policy. Indeed there are no obvious grounds for believing that a sense of national identity will disappear over the next centuries if United Kingdom experience provides a guide. The Scottish and English crowns were united in 1603, the Scottish parliament was abolished in 1707, yet a strong sense of Scottish national identity remains. Even in the absence of a Scottish state or an elected assembly representing the country, Scottish policing and criminal law enforcement differ from the English.[12] By analogy, the organizational, cultural and legal differences between the various police systems of Western Europe are likely to persist for the foreseeable future and few suggest that this is undesirable.

The UK problem is that a sense of European identity has grown slowly in Britain, even though it is well-established in some elites. A

12. The legal frontier between England and Scotland occasionally poses problems for police investigation and criminal prosecutions. See *Problems of Policing the English/Scottish Border,* Association of Chief Police Officers, 1990.

majority of people in Europe, with the exception of the United Kingdom, according to the evidence of the Eurobarometer public opinion surveys, feel themselves to be European as well as French, Spanish, Dutch, Italian and so on. The Maastricht Treaty has established the legal concept of European citizenship by extending the economic and social rights embedded in the Treaty of Rome to political rights (allowing resident EC nationals to vote in local elections), and by giving unrestricted rights of residence (previously restricted to the active population) in all Member States to EC citizens. Most Europeans no longer feel aliens in another European Community country because they are there by right and not as aliens controlled by rules imposed unilaterally by the host country. A European citizenship is, therefore, being developed and it is unlikely that this will meet any serious resistance in the United Kingdom partly because the population has been used to non-British people (citizens of the Irish Republic, and in the past, citizens of Commonwealth countries) voting in British elections and partly because the notion of citizenship has not been well-developed in a country where, until recently, people were 'subjects of the Crown' rather then citizens.

European citizenship implies an enhanced obligation on the part of individuals to assist public authorities of other Member States; the notion of rights without duties is alien to the concept of citizenship. Also, public authorities, including police asking for assistance from their opposite numbers in other EC countries should become equivalent to making the same request within their own state. In the new Europe, it is difficult to argue, as Walzer has done, that the sphere of justice is limited to the boundaries of the state.[13]

All police forces and customs services are inevitably pushed towards closer cooperation to take account of the effects of removal of internal frontier controls on EC citizens and goods of EC origin. All the forces and services have to be trusted to police the external frontier of the EC in a similar spirit, if not in identical ways (a uniform framework for policing the external frontiers is likely to be established in an External Borders Convention but this is bound to leave a large measure of freedom to the individual countries about how they fulfill their obligations). Even the UK, the most unenthusiastic member of the EC about dismantling internal frontiers, is prepared to cooperate fully in the strengthening of the external frontier. Progress has been achieved on common visa policy, common asylum and related matters. It is interesting that the enthusiasm of British customs officers for participating in the Mattheus

13. Walzer M., *Spheres of Justice*, London: Martin Robertson, 1983. His discussion of 'Membership', 31-63, could be applied to the European Community after Maastricht.

programme of exchanges of customs officers in the EC was greater than those of other Member Countries. The 'abolition' of internal frontiers is only possible with trust and mutual support, based on a sense of common purpose and common destiny.

The strengthening of a European identity is an important element of the background to proposals for new kinds of police organization at the EC level as well as establishing a sense of obligation of EC citizens to support the law enforcement authorities of other Member States, about which there still remain traditional suspicions. The development of a sense of identity and common destiny cannot be expected to develop in a smooth linear fashion. It will suffer many setbacks because national and regional interests often conflict sharply and politicians are tempted to use nationalist sentiment to strengthen their own position. It could also be damaged by conflict and inefficiency in the field of law enforcement.

VI. Crime Problems Related to State Security Create Obstacles to Improved Police Cooperation

Although reticences exist at various levels, the goal of improved cooperation is one objective to which all governments subscribe. Although it is generally admitted that police cooperation is only part of a solution (if indeed solutions exist) to certain crime problems, insistence on an arms length relationship with other jurisdictions and a refusal to adapt rules to promote mutual assistance in criminal matters would appear to show a lack of any serious intent to tackle them. This is a reputation which the British government would seek to avoid. In some respects this consensus on objectives remains fragile.

There are particular difficulties in an area in which specifically EC cooperation was initially sought. Terrorism was the stimulus for setting up TREVI but, in Britain and elsewhere, proposals for a European agency for counter-terrorist action, let alone Giscard d'Estaing's suggestion of *une espace judiciaire européenne* to tackle the problem have been regarded as unrealistic in police and law enforcement circles. Although the need for a united front against terrorism has been repeated over and over again in government statements, divisive political considerations play a large role in inter-governmental cooperation in this area. Suspicions can quickly be aroused about the motivations of foreign authorities, the basis of police tactics and the integrity of other countries' jurisdictions and legal procedures. There are many examples, some directly relating to British interests. Failure in 1990-1991 of the

Belgian and Irish authorities to extradite Father Ryan, suspected by the British government of assisting IRA arms procurement, was greeted by a storm of parliamentary protest in the UK. Many foreign observers considered that the chances of a fair trial for Ryan were limited because he appeared to have been tried and found guilty in public parliamentary debate. Similarly the acquittal in 1991 of Northern Irish defendants charged with the murder in the Netherlands of Australian tourists mistaken for British soldiers was widely regarded in the UK as an example of judicial cowardice.

The British are not alone: until the mid-1980s irritation was expressed in official Italian circles about the French 'harbouring' members of the Red Brigades or its off-shoots because French courts would not extradite Italian citizens on vague charges that they were members of an 'armed band'. The Spanish government until 1985 regarded the French authorities' behaviour in treating members of ETA in a manner similar to political refugees as tantamount to abetting the subversion of the young Spanish democracy. There is still evidence of a non-coincidence of views – in February 1992 the French government rejected a Spanish proposal to combat ETA by creating joint Franco-Spanish anti-terrorist brigades, with the possibility of Spanish police exercising executive power on French soil.[14] In general the quality of anti-terrorist cooperation among the Member States of the EC is good but the political dimension of this cooperation inevitably causes conflict. The analysis of the necessary responses to politically motivated violence differs, the priority given to its repression and the appropriateness of the use of certain methods, depending on whether governments are directly involved or not. Also this area highlights the difficult and problematic area of the relations between police and security services. The designation in 1992 of MI5 as the lead agency for domestic anti-terrorist action instead of the police could complicate international cooperation.

VII. The Legal Framework, Rules and Practices of Policing Vary a Great Deal between Countries of the European Communities and there is Opposition to Harmonization in These Areas

In the field of criminal law enforcement (and more generally in home affairs) there are parallels to the timid reactions of thirty years ago about economic integration – structures, mores and relative strengths and

14. *Le Monde*, 29 February 1992.

weaknesses of the various national systems are so different that there are insuperable problems and even dangers in bringing them together. The arguments, which find a ready echo in the United Kingdom, are obvious – there is no common definition of police or police powers throughout the Community because of the divergent legal codes and traditions. The distinction between police and administrative authority is drawn in different ways in different jurisdictions. The police forces report to different authorities and are accountable for their actions in different ways. The police and judicial roles in investigations of crime and criminal law enforcement varies between adversarial and inquisitorial systems. The different criminal procedures of the Member States have a profound effect on the attitudes and behaviour of the police. And so on.

It is difficult for those imbued with English legal and law enforcement cultures, based on precedent and pragmatism, to envisage the possibility of any over-arching harmonization of the European criminal law enforcement systems. But there are piecemeal forms of legal change or harmonization to improve and to extend police cooperation which find support in Britain. Extradition is a major issue on which British official opinion has changed, partly because of the difficulties experienced in extraditing IRA suspects from the Irish Republic and elsewhere. The UK maintained its own cumbersome procedures on extradition, partly because there remained a deep suspicion about foreign jurisdictions and partly because there was pride in the role that Britain played as a secure refuge for political exiles (a role which the present government does not seek to maintain). The UK has proposed to its European partners that there should no longer be a right to refuse extradition on the grounds that a 'political' crime has been committed and, also, that additional charges can be brought after a person has been extradited. The Spanish counter proposal that requests for extradition should be granted automatically, making the handling of these requests an administrative procedure rather than a matter for the courts, received a better press in the UK than the British government's narrower and more pragmatic approach. The civil liberties lobby led by John Wadham, the legal officer of Liberty, strongly protested, asserting that extradition was in itself a punishment and that suspects needed more, rather than less, protection against 'this punishment'.[15]

Harmonization of definition of crimes and of rules of evidence seems a common sense way forward but this immediately confronts basic problems, those of legal concepts and language; legal terms, as they

15. *Independent*, 7 October 1992.

have developed over the centuries, are not readily and accurately to be translated from one European language to another. Language is the vehicle of a legal culture and legal cultures cannot be harmonized by political decision; they can only be subtly blended over time. The difficulties of translating police language, whilst not so severe, are still and important obstacles to efficient cooperation and some of the effort required in this field has already been undertaken.[16]

Different police organizations, disciplines and traditions will not easily be harmonized and will provide obstacles to smooth cooperation at three levels – the political, the professional and the psychological (or cultural). The first arises mainly from the differences between the degree of direct governmental or ministerial control exercised over the police. The British police have been suspicious of the 'political' character of policing in which there is control hierarchy leading directly to the minister. In the professional domain, police training and organizational control are, in part, directed towards the habitual following of certain rules and practices. There is likely to be a difference of view in what is regarded as best practice between those educated and trained in different traditions. The psychological or cultural divide is based on pride in the *corps*, its achievements, traditions and standing. There can therefore be a culture clash between members of different corps in the same country – between metropolitan and provincial forces, between police support units such as the National Criminal Intelligence Service and operational Criminal Investigation Departments, between police and customs law enforcement officers. Domestic inter-agency conflict can affect the quality of cooperation with European arrangements such as Europol. None of these factors is likely to cause insuperable difficulties in coordinated transfrontier police cooperation provided those participating in them are sufficiently sensitive to the problems they pose.

VIII. Unresolved Constitutional Questions Facing the EC and Political Differences about the Progress towards European Union Make Practical Steps towards Improved Police Cooperation Difficult

Four issues with extensive ramifications come under this general heading – the nature of European political union, the tension between defen-

16. *Policespeak; Channel Tunnel Communications Project,* Cambridge: Wolfson College, 1989.

ders of the status quo and reformers, the struggle between bureaucratic interests and the political implications of mistrust of the police.

First – one of the reasons for the British opposition to the inclusion of the word 'federal', despite the obvious federal elements in the Community as it already exists, in the Maastricht Treaty on political union was that it would start to give the EC the characteristics of a state. Any state-like political entity is bound to develop competences in law enforcement and home affairs; the British, and others who thought like them were successful, at least for the moment, in keeping these areas in the domain of inter-governmental cooperation. What this implies for the practice of cooperation has yet to be worked out. But the lack of a clear constitutional destination for Europe is a legitimate reason for caution in police circles about proposals for new exclusively EC systems of police cooperation. The partisans of open government and civil liberties also have some cause for concern about the British insistence on inter-governmental forms of cooperation because these are less transparent, less open and the people concerned in them are less accountable than in the European Community form of cooperation.[17]

Second – there is always a tension between those who argue in favour of the status quo and those who consider change is necessary, between conservatives and reformers. Arguments are always made that new institutions and new organizations are necessary to meet the demands of new circumstances. Politicians come under public pressure to do something about serious problems – institutional reform is often an easy way to respond to critics who argue that not enough is being done, for example, about drugs related offences or organized crime. Chancellor Kohl's initiative on Europol is a good example of a response to public anxieties about the effects of the abolition of internal frontiers in the EC. Against this innovating impulse, persuasive arguments are advanced that the present arrangements can and should be adapted to the new situation and innovations involve costs. The UK government generally adopts this point of view.

Third – political differences are not merely the clash of general views, they also involve bureaucratic interests. Some law enforcement agencies consider the intensification of international cooperation will strengthen their prestige and influence, others fear it will undermine

17. The question of bringing police cooperation within the Community rather than inter-governmental form of cooperation was raised in the European Parliament, Committee on Civil Liberties and Internal Affairs, *Working Document on Police Cooperation*, Rapporteur Mr Van Outrive (OC-EN/DT/205684, 1992), but this suggestion has not figured on the political agenda of governments of the Member States.

their position whilst others have an interest in the status quo.[18] Thus, in European police cooperation, there is a difference of view between those who argue that Interpol exists and its communications facilities can be adapted to take account of closer European union and those who argue that lowering of frontiers and a new distribution of political power requires a new police institution. The former view convinced the British government, at least temporarily, the latter has emerged as the dominant view of the EC Member States after Maastricht.[19] Pragmatically, the British government has aligned itself with the majority view but there is no evidence yet of a strong commitment to it.

Fourth – there is a certain mistrust of the police amongst politicians and ministers. This is an old story and fear of the police has, in the past, led to setting up parallel police forces and other forms of dispersal of police power. In its extreme form, this attitude is expressed as suspicion about any police initiative and action. The attack on the idea of European police cooperation is well exemplified by a meeting of the Greens in the European Parliament, the Greens in the Bundestag and others held on 12 and 13 July 1990.[20] In the United Kingdom, there has been a decline in the traditionally strong trust in the police. The quashing of all the convictions in every major case against people of Irish origin alleged to have participated in terrorist incidents on the UK mainland in the 1970s, the disbanding of the West Midlands serious crime squad and the investigation of CID officers in South Wales for fabricating evidence and other incidents has revealed malpractice which has received wide publicity. The *Independent* newspaper went as far as to characterize the problems of the UK police as 'institutional rot'. This decline in public confidence has no direct connection with closer European police cooperation but it makes informed sections of opinion more wary of any arrangements involving the police which are not transparent and where lines of accountability are unclear. Civil liberties groups and members of the national and European parliaments are uneasy about the development of European police cooperation.[21] It is therefore inevitable that issues concerning police accountability, legal and disciplinary restraints

18. Bigo D., 'L'Europe de la sécurité intérieure; enjeux et rivalités internes dans le processus de formation d'un nouveau champ des activités policières', Paper Presented to the European Consortium for Political Research, Joint Sessions of Workshops, Limerick, 30 March – 4 April 1992.
19. HM Government, *The Government Reply to the Seventh Report of the Home Affairs Committee, Session 1989-1990*, London: HMSO, HC 363-I, Cmd 1367.
20. For a report see *Les Cahiers de la Sécurité Intérieure,* 1990, no. 2, 220-221.
21. For a well-informed British civil libertarian view see Spencer, M., *1992 and All That; Civil Liberties in the Balance,* London: Civil Liberties Trust, 1990.

on police actions, and the procedures for redress if abuses of police powers occur should be the subjects of the liveliest public interest. The British government has not yet seriously addressed the European dimension of these issues.

IX. Advances in European Police Cooperation Are to Be Slow because it Does Not Maintain a Consistently High Place on the Political Agenda and because of the Belief that Existing Systems Can Be Made to Work Better

The three general reasons why pressure builds up for new initiatives in the field of policing are public alarm at certain forms of crime, abuse of police powers or other causes of dissatisfaction with the police, and changes in the structure or functions of government which require a reorganization of the police. The first two scarcely apply in any consistent way in the field of European police cooperation. Crimes such as terrorism and drug-trafficking have an intermittent impact on public opinion and there is no obvious link between them and closer European cooperation; there have been no alarming abuses of police powers in the field of international cooperation.

The greatest pressure for new EC arrangements are the undertakings in the Maastricht Treaty and concern about the effects of the abolition of systematic frontier controls envisaged by the 1992 programme.[22] One British response has been to take advantage of the political weakness of the EC Commission to negotiate an exception from the obligation to cease systematic control of EC nationals at the frontiers. Another response has been to support an existing institution – Interpol. The British official position, in an important Home Office circular concerning international police cooperation, and British parliamentary opinion, expressed in a 1990 report of the Home Affairs Committee of the House of Commons and the government's response to it, moved from apparent indifference to strong support for the Interpol system.[23] Police attitudes

22. A comprehensive review of the issues can be found in House of Lords Select Committee on the European Communities, *1992: Border Control of People,* Session 1990-1991, London: HMSO, 1991; Gregory, F., 'Border Control Systems and Border Controllers; Case Study of the British Police Response to Proposals for a Europe sans frontières', *Public Policy and Administration,* 1991, no. 6, 39-50; Butt Philip, A. 'European Border Controls: Who Needs Them?' London: Royal Institute of International Affairs, 1989, Discussion Paper No. 19.
23. HM Government, *The Government Reply to the Seventh Report from the Home Affairs Committee, Session 1989-90,* London: HMSO, 1991, HC 363-I, Cm 1367.

towards Interpol are generally supportive and most police officers may dismiss Europol as a political gimmick unless it can provide useful services to them.

British support for Interpol illustrates a bias on the part of the policy-making community in the United Kingdom to be more comfortable with global rather than European Community arrangements. This does not necessarily always work against cooperation within the EC because closer intra-EC police cooperation can be enhanced by the application of global or pan-European international treaties. The international legal basis for cooperation in the drugs law enforcement area should be improved by the coming into force (November 1990) of the UN Convention Against Illicit Traffic in Narcotic Drugs and Psychotropic Substances and the opening for signature (11 November 1990) of the Council of Europe Convention on Laundering, Search, Seizure and Confiscation of the Assets of Crime.[24] Political will is, however, required to give substance to the new possibilities of harmonized regimes for both drugs trafficking and money laundering throughout the EC Member States.

Denmark, Ireland and the United Kingdom have not been signatories of the Schengen Agreements.[25] Applying for admission to the Schengen system is unlikely to be a priority of British policy since the UK government has already won an acceptance of its special frontier control regime. However, the Schengen Information System, to which the national police of the member countries will have on-line access, giving information about criminal matters and about unwanted aliens, is clearly a facility which British police forces would find useful. The Schengen rapid response system called SIRENE which will comprise national offices (staffed by lawyers as well as police officers to check on the legality of the action requested), receiving calls for immediate operational action, may upgrade cooperation and the British will be left on one side. Schengen has only been ratified by France and the Lower House of the Netherlands Parliament, but it is likely to be implemented because the contract for the computer facility necessary for the Schengen Information System was agreed in a meeting in Rome in December 1991, and the SIRENE system could be introduced in most countries by

24. Gilmore, W.C., *Going After the Money: Money Laundering, the Confiscation of the Assets of Crime and International Cooperation'*, Edinburgh: University of Edinburgh, 1991, Working Paper 6.
25. For an analysis of the content of the Schengen Agreements and their implications see Den Boer, M., *Schengen: Intergovernmental Scenario for European Police Cooperation*, Edinburgh: University of Edinburgh, 1991, Working Paper 5.

executive action.[26] The British will probably wait to see how the projected European Information System, proposed through TREVI, develops before making public a policy on Schengen.

The momentum to create Europol is now underway and stopping it is not on the agenda of British Eurosceptics. This could change if a proposal was made for direct powers of investigation into crimes against the EC itself, thus prefiguring a genuine federal police force. The *Unité de Coordination de la Lutte Anti-Fraude* (UCLAF) within the EC Commission is a precursor for such a proposal.[27] There is no doubt that fraud against the EC is one factor which creates anti-EC feeling in the UK and there is a belief that other Member States do not take it seriously and may even connive in it. But the dominant view still seems to be that this is a matter exclusively for the law enforcement authorities of the states, and these should be encouraged to take firm action through monitoring procedure.

X. Conclusion

No specific conclusions can be drawn from the wide-ranging *tour d'horizon* of this paper. But three general observations may serve as a conclusion. First, closer European union is legitimated by public support. In the harsh economic climate of the 1990s and the disappearance of the external threat of soviet communism, this support, never strong in the UK, seems to be wavering throughout the Member States of the EC. Police cooperation does not yet have legitimacy beyond the level of passive and ill-informed acceptance; in this respect British opinion is not obviously out of line with that of other European countries. Achieving public support for any form of transfrontier police cooperation has to be worked at and is difficult to achieve. The low public profile of Interpol for many years is a sobering example of the difficulty.

Second, closer European police cooperation is something radically new in the field of law enforcement and has potentially wide political implications. The establishment of Europol runs counter to a British as-

26. A Schengen 'control committee' of the French Senate set up on 26 June 1991 made a highly critical report of the agreements public on 18 December 1991; this was too late to affect the French government's position but may conceivably influence parliamentary opinion in other countries. *Agence Europe* reported a meeting in December 1991 of MPs from the eight countries who have joined Schengen in order better to inform themselves of its implications.
27. Reinke, S., 'The EC-Commission's Anti-Fraud Activity', *European Police Cooperation; Proceedings of a Seminar*, Edinburgh: University of Edinburgh, 1992.

sumption that new institutions at the international level should normally be resisted. In addition, fading belief in the notions such as the sovereignty of parliament, the global responsibilities of the UK, and its presumed status as a great power, maintained by a permanent seat on the UN Security Council, support a traditional desire to keep the widest possible liberty of action in external relations. Most innovations tending to increase functional integration, involving loss of autonomy of the decision making processes of states, have therefore attracted negative reactions from the United Kingdom. However, British pragmatism in policy making usually leads to an acceptance of the radically new if there is no practical alternative.

Third, police services in Britain, as well as others in contemporary Europe, have to retain the support of the populations they serve and this may increase the attraction of closer European cooperation. Policing arrangements as they are require constant explanation and justification. Police malpractice is harshly judged. The police have to be seen to be accountable to clear internal disciplinary procedures, to the courts, and, more generally to democratically elected representatives of the people.[28] If reported crime rates increase, questions are raised about the effectiveness of policing. Faced by these pressures, better European cooperation may be welcomed both by the police as an additional source of legitimacy and of effectiveness in arresting criminals; critics of the police may also support it, as providing institutions which strengthen accountability and control of the police in a world in which transfrontier crime is increasingly common. The challenges in post-Maastricht Europe are clear, the solutions are not yet apparent.[29]

28. These issues are very complex within states. The best recent literature on the UK is Bowden, T., *Beyond the Limits of the Law,* London: Penguin, 1978; Baldwin, R. and Kinsey, R., *Police Powers and Politics,* London: Quartet, 1982; Reiner, R., *The Politics of the Police,* Brighton: Wheatsheaf, 1985; Brogden, M., Jefferson, T. and Walklate, S., *Introducing Police Work,* London: Unwin Hyman, 1988.

29. See den Boer, M., *Police Cooperation After Maastricht,* Hull: University of Hull, 1992, Research Paper No. 2.

Internationalization of Police Cooperation in Western Europe: The German Perspective

Reinhard Rupprecht

I. Introduction

My understanding of the title 'internationalization of the police' is the creation of a European police force, as an institution common to all the EC Countries. There is more than one reason to discuss this issue now and under different national aspects.

Between today and the scheduled date of the abolition of police control at the interior borders in the European Community (EC) there are only a few weeks. The second reason is: we are experiencing a growth in the activities of the mafia, not only in Italy, but also in the urban areas of other European countries. In Germany alone in 1991 68 investigative proceedings were counted which involved mafiosi. The mafia must be seen as a trans-border risk. This is another reason to discuss the necessity and possibility of a European police.

And last but not least: there are differing national views on the issue. They can only be assimilated if they are discussed and analysed in a synopsis.

II. Different National Views

There are indeed different national aspects. These were seen very clearly in the negotiation of the Schengen Agreement and in the TREVI cooperation. On both levels the proposals and agreements concentrated on police cooperation and very seldom dealt with common institutions and international police agencies.

The same divergence of views was experienced in the intergovernmental conference for a European Political Union. It was only Germany which proposed a European police agency at the Luxembourg Summit and it was the German Chancellor, who asked the conference to agree to a Europol with competences in law enforcement.

Different national views are also seen in the TREVI preparatory group for Europol. Some governments are aiming only at a Mini-Europol, a Europol with only coordinating competences or operating only as an information network. There are other governments who favour a Europol with a broad spectrum of non-executive central functions – for example criminal laboratories, common identification systems and so on, and the German government has proposed a Europol with executive functions.

The reasons and roots of these differences are evident.

First of all they are founded on the different history, different cultural developments and different experiences with neighbouring states. The police is – beside the military – the most evident expression of sovereignty. A country like Great Britain without the tradition of a central national police agency is not prepared to accept a European police force. The countries which were occupied during the last World War are very reluctant to transfer police competences to a supranational agency.

The different geopolitical situation also has an impact on the willingness to transfer national sovereignty to international institutions. This willingness is traditionally more to be found on the continent than in island-countries.

According to such differences the national spectrum of views expressed by political parties and other political institutions is different. This also has to do with different levels of criminality (in quality and quantity), with the differing feelings of safety of citizens and with the different levels of acceptance of the police by the general public.

III. No Uniform German View on the Internationalization of the Police

Maybe you would expect a uniform German view on the internationalization of the police despite varying national views. I cannot but disappoint you. It doesn't exist.

There is consensus in all democratic political parties and institutions regarding some principles.

They are all in agreement in their demand that criminal elements should not be able to make profit from the abolition of border control. That means, the qualitative growth of the police forces in Europe should outweigh the loss of security which is a possible consequence of the loss of border controls and of the criminality import from the outer borders of the Community.

There is furthermore full consensus in the view that an internationalization of the police must not reduce the guarantee of civil rights and the substance of the right of informational self-decision or data protection.

And they all agree upon the fact that the principle of subsidiarity must be guaranteed.

Beside these fundamental questions there is no one uniform German view. On the contrary: these views are still in the process of being developed. Nevertheless the tendency to agree to a European police agency with executive competences is in general growing. But we see obvious differences in the emphasis.

The federal government already proposed a Europol with competences for action in the intergovernmental conference of the Luxembourg Summit in June 1991. It was Chancellor Kohl who at the end of the Eighties was the first European 'head' of government to publicly call for the establishment of Europol, and who proposed a treaty commitment to the full to establish a Central European Criminal Investigation Office ('Europol') for these areas by 31 December 1993 at the latest to the European Council in Luxembourg. Details were to be laid down by unanimous decision of the Council concerning the gradual development of Europol functions: first of all it would be a relay station for the exchange of information and experience (up to 31 December 1992), then in the second phase powers to act within the Member States would be granted. There would be a right of initiative for the Commission and also for individual Member States.

This proposal does not address the following questions:

- Should Europol be installed as an EC institution or an intergovernmental agency?
- Should such a European criminal agency investigate alone or only by order of a prosecutor and could such an order be given by every prosecutor, only by the central national prosecution agency or by a European prosecution institution?
- Is it necessary to develop a European penal code and in particular a European criminal procedure code as a base for the investigations of Europol or is the national law a sufficient base for investigative measures of Europol?
- Which are the areas of criminality to be investigated by Europol and what are the other general and special conditions relating to the competence of Europol?
- Should Europol be installed only as a central agency or with field offices in every Member State?

There are a growing number of politicians and experts in Germany calling for a Europol with investigative competences as a consequence of the elimination of border controls and of growing criminality, both organized and international. I mention the Minister of Interior Seiters, the leader of the CDU/CSU-faction in the Bundestag, Dr. Schäuble, and his deputy Gerster, who advocates a Europol as an EC agency with central service functions and field offices and with executive competences. Politicians of the SPD opposition have also proposed Europol.

In Germany all police unions unanimously demand Europol. Hermann Lutz, leader of the biggest police union, the Gewerkschaft der Polizei, underlines the necessity of Europol for policecooperation, and his colleague Freiberg describes the competence of Europol to investigate in cases of organized crime as a long-term aim besides coordination functions and central functions in criminal technics. Harald Thiemann, leader of the German police union Deutsche Polizei Gewerkschaft has just confirmed the goal of creating a Europol with its own search and investigation competences.

I think, however, that the first police union in Germany, which stressed the necessity of Europol, was the Bund Deutscher Kriminalbeamter (BdK). Rolf Jaeger underlined that the BdK has been proposing Europol in the form of an executive police agency since 15 years. On the other hand the UISP bureau (Union Internationale des Syndicats de Police) has just stressed the importance of full parliamentary control of Europol. In its decision of 25 March, 1992, the UISP emphasized the principal competence of national police forces in law enforcement and rejects a European police agency with executive competences. This was also the result of the UISP conference in Granada, last September.

The 16 Bundesländer have a very sceptical view of executive competences of Europol. At a conference in May 1992 they welcomed that the Treaty on European Union includes the institution of Europol, but according to their wish, without executive functions.

There are some radical political parties on the Right and on the Left wing of the political spectrum, which are opposed to the European Political Union: the Republikaner on the one side and the Democratic Socialists Party on the other side. It is easy to understand that these parties do not want a European police agency, in any case not with executive competences.

On the other hand I do not notice any important voice on the German political scene demanding a European police force with more or less unconditional competences, neglecting the principle of subsidiarity and other adequate limitations.

The president of the German Police Academy sees three possible tasks for a European Police Academy:

– Additional studies for the police elite, teaching in particular methods and structures of European police forces, special knowledge and languages;
– Advanced training with respect to all international aspects of police management;
– And an international research strategy: exchange of information, definition of research priorities, coordination and common projects.

IV. A Personal Perspective on Europol

Let me now present my personal perspective on possible – or better: on necessary – functions and competences of an international police agency in Europe on the basis of the proposals made by the federal German government and by the German delegation in the Europol working group of TREVI.

My first remark is: the Schengen system is so far the most comprehensive platform for cooperation in a community of countries. This cannot be stressed often enough, even if the Agreement in question contains a few flaws, e.g. differences in bilateral cross border pursuit arrangements and slowness and limitations related to mutual assistance in law enforcement and extradition.

What I miss especially in the Schengen Agreement is, beside the cooperative element, a strong integrative component. The Schengen Information System (SIS) and the European Information System (EIS) were the only common institutions in the planning until 1991.

Common police institutions of the EC or of the EC Countries would, however, realize more efficiency and lower costs, even without executive power. That is true for:

– The use of technology for police, forensic and customs purposes;
– Research into police science, criminology and criminal investigation techniques;
– Forensic science collections and collections for a identification system;
– Aspects of basic and advanced police training;
– Collection of information of common interest and its analysis for intelligence and police situation reports;
– Security in information technology.

I do not think that there is any need to justify the expediency of such functions in detail. In principle, it is just as obvious as that of the institutions shared by the states in a country with a federal system. For a small federal state to acquire its own scanning electron microscope would make no financial sense, and the same applies to the smaller European countries. The more extensive criminal records and forensic science resources there are, the more useful they are for the purpose of analysis. Why should expensive research be carried out in parallel in more than one country of the Community? It can be more easily financed and used more effectively in common.

It seems to me eminently reasonable that certain areas of basic and advanced police training should be undertaken jointly, such as:

- Certain kinds of advanced training that individual Member Countries cannot undertake on account of the particular specialization concerned;
- Advanced training in the principles of policing in Europe and, above all;
- A one-year joint course leading to a diploma for especially capable senior officers.

The principle of subsidiarity of course applies both to the creation of common institutions and to the unification of internal security functions. A higher level should only be instituted if the lower level is unable to discharge the task as efficiently and rationally.

V. A European Police Force with Executive Powers?

I would like to deal in rather more detail with the area which in the past has met with objections at both national and international level: a European police force with executive powers. This is objected to on both political (the principle of sovereignty) and legal grounds (absence of a European law on policing, a European penal law and a European code of criminal procedure).

A police institution with executive powers would conceivably have two functional areas:

- A European criminal investigation agency that would itself conduct investigations in Member Countries and – possibly
- A European Task Force, that could be used wherever an international hijacking or hostage-taking occurs, involving potential cross-border operations to release the victims; such a Task Force is not as important and necessary, however; it could be substituted by a treaty on cross-border operations in special circumstances.

Why should a police force be necessary in certain circumstances?

The first reason is that the degree of organization and internationalization are increasing steadily in certain fields of criminal activity. The penetration of their organizational ramifications is steadily becoming more difficult. It is all the more important that certain investigatory procedures involving several countries should not only be centrally coordinated but also centrally conducted. The investigation strategy must in such particularly complex and difficult cases be directed by a single center.

Secondly it is not impossible that a national police authority may be unable to investigate a case of internationally organized crime, that also substantially affects partner countries, with the necessary degree of intensity and speed. This risk would be met if Europol were to receive appropriate powers of intervention.

In the third place a Europol institution, equipped with investigatory powers, would set the minds of citizens of European countries at rest and have a deterrent effect on international criminals. These psychological effects should not be underestimated.

In order to correspond to the principle of subsidiarity, Europol's investigatory power must be restricted to cases where important investigations have to be conducted in several countries. They could be limited to certain types of crime that are regularly:

- Perpetrated on an organized basis and consequently are especially difficult to solve; and
- Perpetrated internationally in the sense that the perpetrators originate from different countries or that their crimes involve more than one country.

Europol's investigatory powers may be further restricted to cases where a public prosecutor entrusts an investigation to Europol. A distinction must then in turn be made between national public prosecutors and the creation of a European prosecuting authority. An order given by a national authority for investigations in another country would mean a heavier encroachment on the sovereignty of these countries than granting such powers to a supranational European prosecutor. The latter approach should therefore be preferred.

As far as the problem of the absence of European police law, penal law and code of criminal procedure is concerned, it is certainly unlikely that European law will be created in these areas in the foreseeable future. The EC has no powers of this kind at present. However, these are not really necessary. It may be assumed that Europol would maintain a field office for investigations in each Member Country, and its officers would be from the police forces of that country, i. e. would be familiar with the language and with national law.

VI. Final Remarks

Allow me some final remarks. The creation of common police and prosecuting agencies with investigative competences in a democratic system guaranteeing civil rights demand the following conditions.

First of all full parliamentary control. This control cannot end with the ratification of an intergovernmental treaty or – better – the amendment of the EC treaty by national parliaments. Europol must be controlled by the European Parliament.

The second condition is the guarantee of a high standard data protection. Beside the computerised EIS system Europol will need work files for so called soft personal data with national computer systems. This hopefully intensified exchange of personal data needs at least the same degree of data protection as the national systems.

My third remark is that the creation of a European police is only a segment of European criminal politics and European security politics. These areas of politics are only a part of a necessary common European domestic policy.

Finally, the issue for today is the internationalization of police in Western Europe. It is correct to make a decisive difference between Western and Eastern Europe. Not only because Western Europe forms a denser criminal geographic area, but also because the police system in the Eastern European countries is not as sophisticated as in Western European countries. In accordance with the development of these conditions and of the crime problems, Eastern Europe must be connected with the development of the internationalization of the police forces in Western Europe step by step.

The French Police and Cooperation in Western Europe

Malcolm Anderson

I. Introduction

In the history of European integration, France has been a leading innovator and initiator as well as a source of difficulties and misunderstandings. It is important for future progress that these difficulties are not explained in terms of some nebulous category such as 'national character', which pre-empts a rational discussion of the underlying issues. The strong traditions and practices of the French state and the pressures of domestic politics lie at the root of the chequered, although overall positive, relationship between France and the European Communities. The same general influences will be felt in any system of closer police cooperation in Europe.

In France police investigations and prosecution of criminal offences sometimes encounter difficulties which would not be met in the United Kingdom and, perhaps more rarely, French police find it difficult to cooperate in international enquiries; these may have trivial and contingent explanations but sometimes require analysis in depth of police structures and practices, and the laws regulating them. Mutual comprehension of these structures and practices would assist the organizing of systems of police cooperation as well as facilitating smooth operational cooperation in cases where transfrontier investigations are necessary.

Professional policing in France has a long history and there are historical residues in French police practices which are very tenacious and have had considerable international influence. The organization of French police with a National Police, National Gendarmerie[1] and municipal police forces (usually of little importance for international cooperation) differs markedly from the organization in the English speaking world and some Northern European countries. But it is a model which has influenced thinking about police organization throughout Southern Europe and in many countries in Africa, Asia and Latin

1. Henceforth Police is used to refer to the National Police and Gendarmerie to the National Gendarmerie. When police is used in the lower case it refers to police in general and covers both the Police and the Gendarmerie.

America. This is partly due to the interest aroused in other countries by French policing arrangements from the 18th century and partly due to the influence of the Napoleonic legal code and system of state administration. In recent years the influence of French practices has been actively spread through the training activities and overseas missions of the Service Technique de Cooperation Internationale de Police (STCIP) which is one of the important divisions within the Ministry of the Interior. French police organization has resulted in a specific interface between police and government which has helped to sustain a set of socio-political assumptions about the operation of the police which are unlike those of the United Kingdom. These shaped the nature of police trade unions and professional organizations, and made the internal politics of the police complicated and difficult for the outsider to understand.

The development of the French state, legal code and society has created a complex environment in which police cultures have developed. Attitudes within and towards the police in France are often little more than a sub-set of attitudes towards the state and the exercise of civil authority. But these attitudes should not be regarded as completely stable: rapid social change in the last thirty years has led to a calling into question of some of the entrenched traditional features of the French state. Although old stereotypes die hard, many new ideas have been incorporated into French policing in the last decade. This new flexibility has probably enhanced the potential French contribution to the development of policies and institutions of closer police cooperation in Europe.

However, the ethos, organization and relationship of the French police to the state are highly specific and unlike those of other police agencies, particularly those of Northern Europe. But very different police forces, such as the Royal Canadian Mounted Police and the FBI have cooperated well, and even have on-line access to each other's criminal intelligence files, without apparently having a significant trans-frontier cross-fertilization of ideas on policing policies. It can be argued that French peculiarities are unimportant for closer European cooperation because the police forces of the various countries will be performing the same basic legal and social functions; they therefore, will understand one another well enough without either losing any of their national peculiarities or being strongly influenced by those of others.

I would suggest that this is not the case. If European political union becomes a reality, and the 1991 inter-governmental conferences are putting some flesh on the bones of this aspiration, internal security and control of external frontiers are bound to become priorities for collective

European action. This implies some police facility at the European Community level. One may expect that French ideas and proposals will be very influential in the powers, organization and functioning of this facility. These ideas and proposals will be based on the French experience and understanding of policing. From time to time the ambition to shape the future police system of Europe is expressed openly; a recent book on the French criminal investigation police concluded with the rousing call: 'The French Police Judiciaire (CID) must prepare itself to be the embryo of the French element of the future European CID, in order to be the breeding ground of the essential talent for this new challenge.'[2]

There is, in any case, a gradual move towards harmonization of patterns of policing. The British system of policing is becoming more centralized, the French less centralized; methods of handling criminal intelligence will be harmonized to enable speedy and efficient communication across internal EC frontiers; procedures for communicating evidence between jurisdictions will be streamlined and the arrest of suspects in other countries will be made easier; standardized police terminology, to avoid misunderstanding (already developed bilaterally between the British and the French for policing the Channel tunnel) will come into being, and so on. With closer relations between the European countries, the mutual learning process between police forces which already takes place through bilateral contacts, through Interpol and through Trevi, will accelerate. In all these matters, French assumptions and French ideas will be among the most influential.

It is also important, in the European integration process, that bad police behaviour is not exported from one country to another. In this case, it would be unfortunate if French practices such as the sometimes lethal use of firearms, the cavalier attitude towards telephone tapping, the peculiar interface between politics and the police which produces repeated scandals, and the excessive rivalries between police services spread to other Member States which are not, or are less, affected by them. All countries, however, would do well to look for the motes in their own eye rather to draw too much attention to those of others.

2. Hreblay, V., *La police judiciaire*, Paris: Presses Universitaires de France, 1988, 125.

II. The Long History of the French Police

It would be a mistake to attribute the rigidities of any police institution in the last decade of the twentieth century to the weight of history and tradition and, by doing so, underestimate the highly specific social and political contexts of the present and the recent past. A continuous history of decades or centuries often masks profound change within institutions, and radical modifications in their relations with the environment. However, the sense of having a long history, as well as enduring forms of organization, plays a role in forming attitudes. Further, institutions which have manifestly stood 'the test of time' help to keep proposals for radical change off the agenda.

French professional police forces came into existence at least a century and a half before their nearest English equivalents. Such local arrangements for voluntary and unpaid policing which existed in medieval Europe and which continued in the office of the constable in England were marginalized in France with the extension of royal power, although they continued to exist in the office of the garde champêtre, the forerunner of the municipal police. The Gendarmerie, originally known as the Maréchaussée, dates from the early 13th century but it was increasingly professionalized and given the general mission to police the countryside from the beginning of the 17th century[3]; this mission remains the same. The Paris police was organized under a Lieutenant General of Police in 1667, 162 years before the establishment of the Metropolitan Police in London, and it had a continuous history of three centuries before it was merged with the National Police in the middle 1960s. The French police, have a good claim to be as old as any institution of government in France. In the broader context Bowden writes' France possesses the longest *continuous* system of policing and the most *developed* police tradition in Europe.[4]

The Gendarmerie was officially established in 1791, placed under the authority of the Commissaires de la République (later renamed the Préfets by Napoleon – they briefly resumed their original name under the Socialist government between 1982 and 1986) in 1793, and its organization was defined by a law of 1798. The broad features of the contemporary Gendarmerie were established by an organic decree of 1903 which laid down its relationship with ministerial and administrative

3. *Grand livre d'or historique de la gendarmerie nationale*, Paris: Comité du Monument à la Gloire de la Gendarmerie, 1939; *Gendarmerie nationale; Maréchaussée et gendarmerie; Huit siècles d'histoire*, Paris: Larrien Bonnel, 1967.
4. Bowden, T., *Beyond the Limits of the Law*, London: Penguin, 1978, 140.

authorities, its general duties, and the conditions under which it could engage in the investigation of crimes.[5] The present legal framework of the National Police is of much more recent origin, dating from the law of 9 July 1966 which established the National Police by merging the Prefecture of Police (the Paris police) with the Sûreté Nationale (the police of the provincial towns). The Sûreté Nationale was abolished but the Prefecture of Police continued as a separate service within the National Police with some operational independence but with a common personnel, reduced territory, and fewer independent powers. The Paris police continue to have specific features but there are increasing commonalities with the rest of the National Police, not least because the first posting of many young gardiens de la paix is Paris before they succeed in getting the provincial postings which they much prefer because of better living and working conditions.

The long history of the police has been accompanied by a long tradition of anti-police sentiment, typified by the denunciation by the famous radical intellectual Jean-Paul Sartre of the police as uniformly fascist.[6] The political role of the police, defending the Monarchy under the *ancien régime,* the Empire under Napoleon I against republican and royalist plots, and all the subsequent regimes of the nineteenth century, made the Prefecture of Police in particular thoroughly loathed by opponents of the status quo. Radicals of the Right always thought they had sympathisers inside the police and this was sometimes revealed to be the case; socialists, marxists, syndicalists and other left wing revolutionaries considered the police to be their implacable enemies. This antipathy has undoubtedly been compounded by other factors: 'Traditional mistrust is not based solely on the fact that French policemen are armed, or that members of the CRS (public order police) and Gendarmerie Nationale live in barracks, apart from society. It is based more upon a traditional 'hard' approach to the general public, in which the police have been accused of a disinterested, racist and sometimes brutal approach.'[7] Recent French political history has also complicated the relations between the police and ordinary citizens. The Second World War divided the police, like all other groups and categories of French citizens. Although the Sûreté Nationale lost 713 of its members killed by the

5. For recent history and contemporary organization of the Gendarmerie see particularly Bresson, G. and Rosière, P., *Gendarmerie nationale*, Paris: Xavier Richer, 1982; Haenel, H. and Pichon, R., *La gendarmerie*, Paris: Presses Universitaires de France, 1983; James, J.R., *The French gendarmerie*, Bradford: MCB Publications, 1982.
6. Demonque, P., *Les policiers*, Paris: La Découverte/Maspero, 1983, 6.
7. Hudson, R.C., 'A Matter of Confidence: Police, Public and Society in France since 1981', *Police Journal*, 1988, no. 2, 169-174.

Germans and the Gendarmerie lost 750, there were others who sided with the Vichy regime and collaborated, with varying degrees of enthusiasm, with the Germans in rounding up Jews and Communists, and combating the Resistance. Legal action is now (in 1991) being taken against the Vichy director of police for complicity in war crimes. The Liberation period of 1944-1945, with conditions of latent civil war and an indiscriminate purge of collaborators, was a traumatic period for the police and its standing with the public revived only slowly. It had not completely recovered when the most dramatic episode in decolonization, the Algerian war (1954-1962), brought political violence to France and deeply divided French opinion. Although there were some sympathisers in the police with the last ditch defence of French Algeria, the main problem was allegations of political bias. Whether or not the police took action against the Algerian nationalists and their supporters or the militant and violent defenders of French Algeria, they were accused of being politically partisan. There were also police shootings and infringements of civil liberties which are the almost inevitable accompaniment of violent and confused political situations.

The effects of the Algerian war were surprisingly short-lived but the police (particularly the public order police) were plunged into another political maelstrom – the students' uprising and the general strike of 1968. The students' revolt was in one respect a triumph of policing; despite the scale of the disorders, there was no loss of life until it was virtually over. The events of May 1968, however, marked the alienation of the police from a whole generation of educated young people. Many of the working class groups which took part in the general strike, and particularly those who adhered to revolutionary ideologies, were already deeply alienated from the police. This is partly because of the tradition of robust policing of strikes in France which goes back to the 19th century and partly because of the vulgar marxist belief that the police are the instrument of an oppressive capitalist class. The relative decline of violence in strikes and the ebbing of marxist ideology has resulted in some improvement in trade union-police relations. However, the traditional working class has been replaced by a new alienated group – the large, mainly north African, immigrant groups. Urban violence in recent years, which have caused considerable policing problems and much criticism of the police, has mainly centred on the deprived areas of the large cities where the immigrants live.

III. The Organization of the Police and the Gendarmerie

Despite recent measures directed towards political and administrative decentralization, the French police system remains highly centralized under direct ministerial control. Although the concept of the police function has been narrowed over the last two hundred years, it remains a broad one compared with other European countries, particularly through the wide definition given to the legal concept of *ordre public* which includes the maintenance of tranquillity, security and salubrity against threats or potential threats.[8] These features made French policing anathema to English liberals in the 19th century and some of this antipathy remains.

The original mission of the French Police and Gendarmerie was as the essential arm of the secular power, to preserve public order and security, and the interests of the French monarchy or, what was coming to be called in the 17th century, the state. Maintaining the authority of the state, what Brodeur calls 'high policing' as opposed to 'low policing' (ordinary crime control), was established as the dominant priority at an early date.[9] This priority survives in the two national forces, in their organization and their responsibilities. There is a strict hierarchy in both the Police and the Gendarmerie which leads up to the minister in Paris. Both have complex structures and the first organization chart is intended to provide a simplified comparison of their hierarchies; the second organization chart is of one service of the Police, the Police Judiciaire – criminal investigations service, to give some impression of the complexity of their internal organization. Both Police and Gendarmerie have strong, by British standards, public order police reserves; both have a role of gathering intelligence related to state security in counter-espionage and in counter terrorism.[10]

In the case of the Gendarmerie, under the control of the Ministry of Defence and integrated into the military command structure, there is no separation of the police and the military function. Dubbed the first regiment of the French army, it has a military hierarchy with military ranks and territorial commanders at the regional départemental and cantonal levels; with planes, helicopters and armoured vehicles it is capable of serving as a light military fighting force if the need arises. The Gendar-

8. Picard, E., *La notion de police administrative*, Paris: Librairie Général de Droit et de Jurisprudence, 1983.
9. Brodeur, J.P., 'High Policing and Low Policing; Remarks about the Policing of Political Activities', *Social Problems*, 1983, no. 5, 507-520.
10. The Gendarmes Mobiles, and the Compagnies Républicaines de Sécurité of the Police with a combined strength of about 30,000.

merie also assists in the enforcement of military law and discipline; they escort military convoys and perform duties which are usually done by military police in other countries. The Police have no role in these areas.

Involvement of Gendarmerie (and, in a marginal way, the Police) in military tasks is often misleadingly considered, in English speaking countries, as a symptom of immaturity in police systems. In a country like France with, in the recent past, deep social and political divisions, where the constitutional order was always at risk, and where subversion as well as military attack could be mounted across land frontiers, an enhanced paramilitary as well as an intelligence role for the police is generally accepted. In recent British imperial history the distinction between army and police has been blurred in Ireland, Cyprus, Palestine and India for broadly similar reasons. Arguments have also been made that there is an increasing paramilitary element in the British police since the 1970s.[11] The declining threat of subversion in France is calling into question some of the paramilitary aspects of the 'soldiers of the law,' the gendarmerie. However, making one institution, the Police Nationale, which has many critics, responsible for the whole national police system is not likely in any future which can be foreseen.

As with the majority of police forces world-wide, both the Gendarmerie and the Police are highly rule-bound organizations and both provide their members with rule books which are supposed to cover virtually all contingencies. The use of firearms by the Police is particularly subject to stringent rules although this does not prevent incidents occurring. Each gendarme has a *Mémento du gendarme,* a six hundred page loose-leaf book giving information and instruction on detailed and often apparently trivial matters – the approach to be adopted to the problem of a damaged fence, the proper labelling of a box of oysters and similar matters.[12]

In terms of discipline and accountability there are differences between the two organizations although strict accountability to hierarchical superiors and accountability to the *juge d'instruction* (examining magistrate) when they are acting as criminal investigators are common principles to them both. Both are subject to the ordinary law when accused of criminal offences such as unlawful killing. But the Gendarmerie conforms to the usual model of military discipline with frequent inspections and summary discipline by commanding officers for trivial

11. Jefferson, T., *The Case against Paramilitary Policing,* Milton Keynes: Open University Press, 1990.
12. Regan, D., 'Police Status and Accountability: A Comparison of the British, French and West-German Models', ECPR, 1984, Paper no. 20.

offences and courtsmartial for more serious ones. The Police has an internal system of administrative discipline which in principle has more safeguards for the rights of the accused and is carefully monitored by the Police unions. Both have internal policing systems in the form of Inspectorates General attached to the Directors' General offices. The Inspectorate General of the Police is constantly criticized by the Police unions, representing the lower ranks, for allegedly not respecting the rights of police under investigation.[13]

This complaint may well be justified but it commands little public sympathy because police often seem to lack respect for the rights of individuals suspected of offences or who merely happen to be in the vicinity of offences when there are committed. The right to silence is not effectively guaranteed in French law and in 'on the scene of crime' investigations police officers questions must be answered.[14] The principle of *habeus corpus* is not always respected and it is not unknown for witnesses as well as suspects to be arrested; unauthorized phone tapping is a longstanding and continuing scandal. Also, the system of public complaints against the police either through the public prosecutors' office or directly to the Inspectorate General has low credibility and this does not help police who complain about their own treatment.[15] Allegations of racism and brutality often seem either to be ignored or not investigated in a way which is satisfactory to the complainants.

Whether the public suspicion of the way in which complaints against the police are handled is justified or not is difficult to assess. The statistics for the 1980s published in the annexes to two recent books can be read in different ways.[16] Violent acts by members of the Police seldom result in administrative punishments or convictions in the courts because the facts are rarely established. The number of private individuals complaining directly to the Inspectorate General of Services (IGS) for Paris and the Inspectorate General for the Police (IGPN) for the whole country, rather than to the judicial authorities, was increasing in percentage and absolute terms in the second half of the 1980s. Although this was a reversion to a similar proportion a decade earlier, it could denote

13. See Ancian, J.-M., *La police des polices*, Paris: Balland, 1988.
14. Stefani, Levasseur and Bouloc, *Précis de procédure pénale*, Paris: Dalloz, 1987, 13th editon.
15. Ancian, J.-M., *La police des polices*, Paris: Balland, 1988; Léauthier A. and Ploquin, F., *Les flics; 120,000 inconnus*, Paris: Flammarion, 1990; Gleizal, J.J., *Le désordre policier*, Paris: Presses Universitaires de France, 1985.
16. Ancian, J.-M., *La police des polices*, Paris: Balland, 1988, 225-236; Léauthier, A. and Ploquin, F., *Les flics; 120,000 inconnus*, Paris: Flammarion, 1990, 287.

either an increase in confidence in the IGS or an increased propensity to complain. Although many enquiries are initiated few members of the Police are actually convicted after a trial. For example in 1987, the IGS dealt with 1,306 cases, opening an enquiry on 746, more than a third of which resulted in internal disciplinary action (234); only 58 police officers were found guilty by the courts and 39 of these for off-duty activities. In some of the most publicized cases the Inspectorates do not intervene and the sanctions imposed do not always seem proportionate to the offence.

The Police are subject to some civilian control at the local and regional level because the maires of communes have police powers which they can exercise directly through locally recruited police (municipal police) under the supervision of the préfet; the préfet himself as the agent of the Minister of the Interior and the titular head of all state services in the regions and the départements also has important police powers exercized particularly in emergencies. Maires and préfets do not, as a general rule, intervene in operational matters. Reforms of the early 1980s, in particular by Prime Minister Mauroy of the National Council for Crime Prevention and, more especially the Communal Councils for Crime Prevention have established new and closer contacts between the public, elected officials and the Police.

The organization of the Gendarmerie and the Police differ in many respects but one notable feature in common is the existence of an officer class. Both the Gendarmerie and the commissaires of the Police have a direct entry to the officer corps. The commissaires usually have a law degree but just over half are recruited from the next level down in the hierarchy, the officier de paix (uniformed) or inspecteur (plain clothes) grades, usually with many years service; both direct entry and promoted commissaires are trained at the Ecole Nationale Supérieure de Police at Saint Cyr au Mont d'Or in the suburbs of Lyon. Gendarmerie officers are trained with other military officers at the elite military academy of Saint Cyr and at the Ecole des Officiers de la Gendarmerie Nationale at Melun (there is also provision for promotion from the non-commissioned ranks between the ages of forty to forty six). An additional way in which hierarchical relationships are entrenched is that the various levels of the Police and Gendarmerie have differing legal powers in their dealings with the public. In educational background, experience, legal powers, and pay and conditions commissaires and Gendarmerie officers are separated from the other ranks.

Bernard Deleplace, the former secretary general of the FASP, has eloquently described the disdain with which commissaires often treat the gardiens de la paix (the lowest rank of the Police) and the strained and unsympathetic relations which result.[17] The FASP conducted a survey, published in *Le Monde,* 10 August 1987, which showed that 64% of gardiens de la paix believed that the existing hierarchical relations were damaging for the efficient conduct of police functions; among the public order police (the Compagnies Républicaines de Sécurité) the proportion reached 81%. Among the discontented 60% thought that this resulted in poor coordination and 49% in poor organization of command. The plain clothes detectives union circulated in 1988 to its members an assessment form for their commissaires based on the annual assessment form which the commissaires completed for the detectives.[18] As well as the usual questions, the questionnaire contained questions relating to grievances against their superiors – unauthorized time off, cultivating the local politicians and doing their bidding, use of police vehicles (or petrol coupons) for private purposes, style of leadership (from the front without consultation or from behind to escape responsibility), 'surprising' use of public funds and so on. The clear impression was that the rules which were strictly applied to the lower ranks were not applied to their superiors. This criticism of the top of the hierarchy by the base is to be expected and it is not unusual. However, the hierarchical organization and attitudes of a previous period seem to have survived into a social, political and professional environment in which they are no longer appropriate and are difficult to tolerate.

The most striking feature of the professional life of the police forces is the intense rivalry between the National Police and the National Gendarmerie. This has persisted throughout the 19th and 20th centuries and has perhaps been deliberately fostered by governments as a means of controlling them or in order that one or the other does not become too powerful.[19,20] Each tends to believe that governments favour the other. Three commissions have attempted, without apparent success, to propose solutions for the tension between the Gendarmerie and the Police.[21] Rivalry within the Police between various services is sometimes intense and can compromise some investigations and operations. In some instances and places, such as Marseilles, this has been a serious and conti-

17. Deleplace, B., *Une vie de flic*, Paris: Gallimard, 1987.
18. *Le Monde*, 25/26 August 1988.
19. Casamayor, *La police*, Paris: Gallimard, 1973.
20. Loubet del Bayle, J.-L., 'La police francaise en 1984', Paper Presented to the European Consortium for Political Research, Joint Sessions of Workshops, 1984.
21. The Tricot commission of 1972, the Racine commission of 1979 and the Cabannes commission of 1987.

nuing problem.[22] The rivalry between services has sometimes been provoked or exacerbated by the changing law enforcement priorities of the government. Under the Chirac government (1986-1988), the priority given to the issue of illegal immigrants, undocumented foreigners, and dealings with foreign governments and intelligence agencies over hostages increased the profile of the Police de l'Air et des Frontières, Renseignements Généraux and the Direction de la Surveillance du Territoire and downgraded the Police Judiciaire and the uniformed police.

Apparently small issues can provoke major confrontations between Police and Gendarmerie such as the circular of 11 May 1987 from the director of the Gendarmerie specifying the conditions in which gendarmes are authorized to work in civilian clothes. The point at issue was the tension between the Police and the Gendarmerie over criminal investigation work – if the gendarmes could, as a matter of course, perform plainclothes duties, they would intrude still further into the territory regarded by the Police as its own. There was a closing of the ranks of National Police unions. A joint press conference was held by the Syndicat National des Hauts Fonctionnaires et Commissaires de Police (SNC), the Syndicat National Autonome des Policiers en Civil (SNAPC), the main union for the detectives and inspectors, and the Syndicat des Commandants et Officiers (SCO). The Secretary General of the SCO, Daniel Dugléry, said: 'The idea of a militarized police which performs duties in civilian dress should be rejected. The fight against crime and delinquency should not be used progressively to implement measures which are dangerous for liberty'.[23] The wearing of civilian dress for surveillance and for investigations where the sight of a uniform could compromise the chances of success had been standard practice for many years. But this was the first time that it had been the subject of a formal circular; the justification for the circular was to set guidelines for a matter which previously had been left to local discretion. The Police complained that it was not consulted (the Ministry of Defence regarded it as a matter of internal regulation of the Gendarmerie); the result was a public dispute between the Minister of State responsible for the Police, Robert Pandraud, and the the Minister of Defence, André Giraud.[24]

Behind this ideological quarrel lies a struggle for territory. The countryside and small towns, the territories of the gendarmes, have suf-

22. Léauthier, A. and Ploquin, F., *Les flics; 120,000 inconnus*, Paris: Flammarion, 1990, 70-73.
23. *Le Monde*, 6 June 1987.
24. As under 23 *supra*.

fered a dramatic decline in population, commencing in the mid 19th century and accelerating after the Second World War. Rural France was even shrinking physically as the urban population grew. The Gendarmerie, therefore, have sought to maintain themselves in urban areas even when they grow beyond the 10,000 threshold at which point the Police are supposed to take over. The Gendarmerie have also sought to extend their criminal investigation functions to the towns. There is no statutory reason why they should not and many examining magistrates have used their services rather than those of the Police. The Police regard this as improper competition; they argue that the frontiers between the two organizations should be clearly defined, otherwise there would be conflicts of competence and serious incidents between the Police and plainclothes gendarmes. Incidents had already occurred in which the Police and the gendarmes had taken each other as criminals.[25] This was followed by a report by the General Inspectorate of the National Police published on 19 February 1988 which sharply criticized the expansionary policy of the gendarmes and accused them *inter alia* of laying siege to examining magistrates to obtain authority to investigate cases.[26]

When the Socialists regained a parliamentary majority in 1989, the Minister of the Interior, Pierre Joxe, announced that he intended to put an end to the tension between Police and Gendarmerie. As Minister of Defence in 1990 he stated that he was very well placed to continue his efforts in this direction.[27] He asserted that the directors of the Police and Gendarmerie had started to work closely together and he proposed a bill in April 1991 clarifying the competences of the Police, Gendarmerie and Customs. There had been other signs of progress, such as the representation of the Gendarmerie in the National Central Bureau of Interpol which hitherto had been regarded as a preserve of the Police. Pierre Joxe has proposed in May 1991 a bill to regulate the relationship between the Gendarmerie, Police and Customs. In this, he has at least the passive support of public opinion which, from the late 1960s has wished to see a merger of the Police and Gendarmerie.[28] Unless there is a major scandal or confrontation, a merger is unlikely because it would involve a complete change in the characteristics of the Gendarmerie, a loss to the Ministry of Defence of a major responsibility and an change in the bureaucracy and the vested interests of its members which has only

25. Report in *Le Monde*, 10 August 1987.
26. At present the Gendarmerie deal with about a third of the investigations of crimes and indictable offences – *La gendarmerie nationale en bref*, Paris: La Documentation Francaise, 1991, 4.
27. *Le Monde*, 5 February 1991.
28. Le Clère, M., *La police*, Paris: Presses Universitaires de France, 1972, 11.

been experienced in times of revolutionary upheaval. However, in a more closely integrated Europe, the militarized police forces of Southern Europe may come to seem increasingly anachronistic.

IV. Police Culture

There is much theory and debate about the culture of complex organizations but since there is very little systematic research data on French police culture(s), a deliberately naive approach is adopted here. Culture can be taken to mean values (concerning authority, individual and collective responsibility, freedom and order), perceptions (how the police system works, how police relate to the government and to the public) and attitudes (towards the hierarchy, colleagues, complainants, forms of policing and types of criminality). Culture informs all aspects of police work – the spirit in which rules are applied, how people view their colleagues and people outside their service or organization and the sources of inspiration in situations in which rules are not applicable.

There are broadly two diametrically opposed views of the significance of police cultural patterns within and across national boundaries. The first is that policing is a basic social function and police officers confront very similar situations and problems; behind all the differences of language, tradition and political system, very similar cultural patterns emerge.[29] The second is that different historical experiences, different political ideologies and different legal orders sustain mutually incomprehensible and perhaps incompatible patterns of values and attitudes; very different police cultures can exist in the same country and at different levels in the same police service; this has the potential of making cooperation and coordination between police services difficult as, for example, between the Police and the Gendarmerie in France.

Cultures are deeply embedded in language and a close analysis of the discourse of the French police is a necessary (but as yet unresearched) preliminary to a study of police culture. The language of the Police is rich and colourful. It can be sampled in the books written by ex-policemen but it is often unclear whether the vocabulary has been borrowed from or has been taken over by writers of detective stories.[30] The

29. Punch, M., *Policing the Inner City; A Study of Amsterdam's Warmoesstraat*, London: Macmillan, 1979; Mawby, R.I., *Comparative Policing Issues; The British and American System in International Perspective*, Hemel Hemstead: Unwin Hyman, 1990.
30. Gévaudan, H., *'Ennemis publics'; Mes grandes enquetes criminelles*, Paris: Lattès, 1989; Morèas, G., *Ecoutes et espionnage*, Paris: Stock, 1990; Pellegrini, C. and De Monpezat, E., *A chacun sa mort*, Paris: Editions No. 1, 1990; see also Léauthier, A. and

terms can be quickly learned – *filoches* = *filatures* (shadowing by a detective), *sonnettes* = *équipe de surveillance* (surveillance team), *zonzons* = *écoutes téléphoniques* (telephone taps), *tontons* = *indicateurs* (informants), *sucette* = *récepteur-émetteur* (walky-talky), *camembert* = *bandes de magnétophone pour les écoutes* (recording tapes) – but the mental universe which they partly express and partly constitute is less easy to penetrate. Very little anthropological or sociological work in France has been done because of the gulf which separates the police from academic and intellectual milieu – there is only one research based publication on the political culture of the commissaires, one local study of police culture and an interesting but impressionistic chapter in a book by a psychologist.[31,32,33]

Several strands within French police culture clearly exist. The world of the plain clothes criminal investigator, captured in the three books referred to above (Gévaudan 1989, Moréas 1990, Pellegrini, Monpezat 1990) is the best known but it is hard to sift myth from reality in the thrill of the chase, the confrontation with the villain, and the almost obligatory touch of admiration for the major professional criminal.[34] For other branches of the police and uniformed police of all ranks, the sources on which an analysis of police culture may be based are sparse, comprising some autobiographies and impressionistic works which are

Ploquin, F., *Les flics; 120,000 inconnus*, Paris: Flammarion, 1990, 79.

31. Portelli, G., *Portrait socio-culturel des commissaires de police*, Toulouse: Institut d'Etudes Politiques de Toulouse, 1987.
32. Guillermou, G., *Contribution à l'analyse de la culture policière: Le cas des polices urbaines*, Tours: Université Francois Rabelais de Tours, 1989.
33. Lhuilier, D., *Les policiers au quotidien; Une psychologue dans la police*, Paris: L'Harmattan, 1987, Chapter 2. The absence of an academic literature on the police is frequently deplored. The political science literature (according to Journès, C., ed., *Police et politique*, Lyon: Presses Universitaires de Lyon, 1988, 8-9) is limited to two books by Gleizal, J.J., *La police nationale*, Grenoble: Presses Universitaires de Grenoble, 1974 and *Le désordre policier*, Paris: Presses Universitaires de France, 1985; an article by J-L., Loubet del Bayle J-L., 'La police dans le système politique francais', *Revue Francaise de Science Politique*, 1981, 509-534; a chapter in a book by Birnbaum, P., *La logique de l'etat*, Paris: Fayard, 1982, chapter 3; references in a book by Quermonne, J-L., *Les régimes politiques occidentaux*, Paris: Seuil, 1986, and two special numbers of reviews: *Procès*, 'Histoire comparée de la police', 1984, nos. 15-16, and *Revue de Sciences Politiques*, 'Police', 1984, nos. 16-17. Loubet del Bayle, J-L., (*Police et société*, Toulouse: Presses de l'Institut d'Etudes Politiques de Toulouse, 1988, 14-17) deplores, in more detail and with more authority, the relative paucity of sociological works on the police in France. The establishment by the Minister of the Interior, Pierre Joxe, of the Institut des Hautes Etudes de Sécurité Interne (IHESI) will bring much needed resources to police studies.
34. Gévaudan, H., *'Ennemis publics'; Mes grandes enquêtes criminelles*, Paris: Lattès, 1989; Pellegrini, C. and De Monpezat, E., *A chacun sa mort*, Paris: Edition No.!, 1990; Moréas, G., *Ecoutes et espionnage*, Paris: Stock, 1990.

now often too dated to be of contemporary value, journalists and the excellent articles in *Le Monde* by Georges Marion and Laurent Greilsamer.[35, 36]

The general environmental factors which help to shape police values, attitudes and perceptions are fairly clear. In this context it is not possible to do more that list them. The *first* is the long hierarchy and the relatively distant relations, both personal and professional, between various levels of the hierarchy. It is sometimes difficult for hierarchical authority to be exercized effectively and each chief of section and service tends to try to preserve autonomy and independence.[37] This phenomenon noticed and analyzed in Michel Crozier's general work on bureaucracy has survived less changed in the police than in other branches of the French state.[38] The sense of vocation and professional ethos, and the whole mental universe of police officials differs in the senior, middle and lower ranks of the police. The *second* is the position of the Police as servants of the state and the conviction, maintained by the code of criminal procedure, that this marks the Police off from their fellow citizens. The Police are civil servants whose administrative acts are subject to administrative law and who have certain rights as civil servants such as the right to form unions but not the right to strike. They are also members of one of the well-established corps of the French state and like the other corps are highly, and usually effectively, resistant to unwelcome change imposed from the outside. The *third* is the awkward position of serving three masters – the political master (the minister, his *cabinet* and the head of the Police or Gendarmerie who is always a civilian appointment). the professional master (corps which have developed over the years a highly complex organization and set of rules which ministers can have great difficulty in controlling or changing and which dominate most police men and women's working lives) and the judicial master (the Minister of Justice and the hierarchically organized magistrature which controls all investigations and the establishment of evidence).

35. E.g. Sicot, M., , *Grandeurs et servitudes policières; Quarante ans à la Sureté*, Paris: Productions de Paris, 1959; Manceaux, M., *Les policiers parlent*, Paris: Seuil, 1969; although see Ottavioli, *Echec au crime*, Paris: Grasset, 1985; Harstrich, J. and Calvi, F., *R.G.; 20 ans de police politique*, Paris: Calman-Lévy, 1991.
36. Ancian, J.-M., *La police des polices*, Paris: Balland, 1988; Léauthier, A. and Ploquin, F., *Les flics, 120,000 inconnus*, Paris: Flammarion, 1990.
37. Gleizal, J.J., *Le désordre policier*, Paris: Presses Universitaires de France, 1985.
38. Crozier, M., *The Bureaucratic Phenomenon*, Chicago: University of Chicago Press, 1964.

The *fourth* is the rivalry between police services. The major source of friction between the Police and the Gendarmerie has already been emphasized in the previous section. But there is often an equally virulent rivalry between the operational services of the Police and between Police and Customs whose relations are sometimes very bad. This 'guerre des polices', frequently denounced by the police themselves, often becomes public; versions of disputes between police agencies are published in the newspapers, sometimes as a result of leaks from the warring parties.[39] This affects police attitudes towards their colleagues in other services and the degree to which they think they can be trusted. The *fifth* is the attitude of the public to the police. The level of public satisfaction in France reported in the opinion polls is open to varying interpretations. On the one hand, public confidence in the police is at a lower level than in countries such as Britain and Denmark but it is higher than for most other French institutions and has been rising in the 1980s.[40] On the other hand, the perception of the commissaires is that more people have feelings of mistrust and fear of the Police than trust them.[41] Ambivalent attitudes towards the Police are partly the legacy of a politically and socially troubled history, partly the public perception that the police are there to repress and control rather than to provide assistance, and partly because the great publicity given to poor police conduct – conduct which persistently recurs despite some firm calls to order by ministers.

The *sixth* is the male domination of police services; the entry of women came first as auxiliaries in the early 1970s and then as full police officials (Gardiens de la Paix 1978), able to carry arms and have the same obligations as men, in both the Police and Gendarmerie. Recruitment of women increased rapidly from 957 to 4,326 in all ranks between 1981 and 1987 but this represented only an increase from 1% to 4% of the total number of police officers.[42] The male ethos of the police is likely to persist for many years. In the 1980s recruiting publicity still carried the slogan 'La police un métier d'hommes' before being changed later in the decade to 'La police un métier d'avenir'. Quotas on

39. Ottavioli, *Echec au crime*, Paris: Grasset, 1991, 335-352 gives a balanced and informed view.
40. Maurin, J.L., in: Loubet del Bayle, J.-L. et al., *Police et société*, Toulouse: Presses de l'Institut d'Etudes Politiques de Toulouse, 1988, 21-38.
41. Portelli, G., *Portrait socio-culturel des commissaires de police*, Toulouse: Institut d'Etudes Politiques de Toulouse, 1987, 234.
42. Fore more statistics see Léauthier, A. and Ploquin, F, *Les flics; 120,000 inconnus*, Paris: Flammarion, 1990, 286.

the female intake were dropped as being contrary to EC law but in 1989 the Ministry of the Interior raised the minimum height for entrants to the Police from 1.63 metres to 1.66 metres, thus excluding 70% of women. The *seventh* is the emergence of practices which have analogies in all large organizations, and which may transgress internal rules and, in extreme cases, are illegal. An example of the latter was the systematic payment of bogus travel expenses, allegedly to cover out of pocket expenses which could not be easily claimed; the plain clothes inspecteurs union, the SNAPC, had long campaigned against this practice probably because the commissaires received the lions' share of these expenses; it was not until the middle 1980s that the matter came to a head when brought before a parliamentary enquiry, after refusals to accept these payments by some junior officers. These practices are significant because they can lead to acceptance of a selective approach to law enforcement. There is inevitably some police discretion about whether to enforce laws although, in principle, French law allows no discretion because police officers can be sanctioned if they know that an offence has been committed by a specific person and they fail to take action. However, if internal rules are consistently ignored it could encourage similar attitudes towards certain laws.

These pressures can produce a peculiar mixture of cynicism and sense of public duty; a belief in the legitimacy of pursuing private and sectional interests yet a developed concept of the public or state interest; deference mixed with insolence towards superiors and members of other corps; ignoring of certain instances or forms of law breaking yet a tenacious pursuit of some criminal conspiracies; rigid adherence to rules yet a rather cavalier attitude to some laws if they hinder criminal investigations. These and other attitudes and values exist in different combinations in different parts of the police.

Perhaps the most difficult and intriguing dimension of police culture is the political attitudes of police officials. It is widely assumed in France that the police, because of their repressive role and their function of maintaining order in society, are almost always Right wing in their views. The detailed study by Portelli (1987) of the attitudes of the commissaires supports this view. It is reinforced by expressions of police hostility to Left wing governments. Over 2,000 police officers, many in uniform engaged in an illegal anti-government demonstration in 1983 to show their anger at what they regarded as the Socialist government's neglect of the police and its lax attitude towards criminals.[43] But this government had shown an unusual interest in police reform; in 1982, the Socialist Minister of the Interior launched a plan for the modernization of the French police, introducing ideas of more community based policing in France for the first time. This initiative showed that there was a constituency in the Police in favour of progressive reform. The modernization plan was warmly welcomed by the largest police organization, the FASP, mainly composed of the unions of the lower ranks. The lower profile Union des Syndicats Catégoriels (USC) which, at the time, grouped most of the unions of the senior ranks and is more Right wing in orientation, remained silent.

The responses of the Police to the Socialist government and 'top-down' reform in general shows the complexities of police professional organization – there are over twenty police unions. For example, the FASP includes the Syndicat National des Commissaires (SNC), the smaller of the two unions representing the commissaires; the other is the Syndicat des Hauts Fonctionnaires et Commissaires de la Police (SCP) which is in the USC.[44] The largest and most important member of the FASP is the Syndicat Général de la Police – SGP (representing the lowest ranks of the uniformed Police – the gardiens de la paix). Although the police unions for the most part avoid party political links and associations, the FASP under the leadership of Bernard Deleplace was close to the Socialists. A persistent extreme Right wing strand survives in the lower ranks of the Police represented by the Fédération Professionelle Indépendante de la Police (FPIP). The FPIP publishes a periodical *Police et Sécurité* which expresses views close to Le Pen's Front National. It accuses the Republican regime of lack of effectiveness in the fight against terrorism and crime; denounces academics, cosmopolitan intellectuals, immigrants, Left wing politicians (described as anti-French racists), journalists, and television reporters; and recommends solidarity with policemen who have drawn their guns and killed people suspected of wrong-doing.[45]

Similar reactionary attitudes have been present in the police since the emergence of a populist extreme Right in the later 19th century but they

43. This demonstration was dwarfed on the next occasion that the Police took to the streets. In May 1991 a legal demonstration to protest about pay and the (still) slow pace of modernization of the Police attached an estimated 15,000 for two seperate marches in Paris (*Le Monde*, 24 May 1991).
44. The USC was partially supplanted in October 1990 by the new Fédération Nationale Autonome de la Police and the SCP decided to join the new Federation (*Le Monde*, 17/18 March 1991).
45. *Le Monde*, 11 September 1986.

are rejected vigorously by other minorities and disapproved of by the great majority of the police. The Confédération Démocratique du Travail (CFDT) – Police made numerous representations to encourage action against what it described as the 'anti-constitutional' character of the FPIP.[46] Other unions restricted themselves to conventional platitudes about excluding partisan politics from the Police – a platitude also used by the SCP to denounce the neo-socialism of the FASP.

The police are therefore divided politically and their professional organizations are fragmented and faction-ridden.[47] The divisions seldom seem to be directly linked to issues of pay, although there are hidden agendas about differentials. According to Georges Marion, a very well informed journalist, if one listened to the police unions the main concerns of the police are not pay and pensions but the condition of their service and the nature of their mission.[48] The ideal terms in which the police conceived their profession and the drab everyday reality of police work were in painful contrast; a survey of the Paris police stations by the Syndicat Général de la Police (SGP) reported in 1987 provided abundant illustration of this.[49]

The Gendarmerie has no trade unions as these are forbidden within the armed forces but the malaise of the Gendarmerie of the summer of 1989, was based on grievances similar to those revealed by the survey of the Police in 1987. Lacking trade unions, the gendarmes resorted to anonymous manifestos in the press and in semi-public grumbling; these reached a pitch which compelled the government to take notice and the Minister of Defence was obliged to listen personally to grievances expressed by the 'other ranks'. The grievances focussed on the equipment of the Gendarmerie, long working hours, poor working conditions and relations with the officer corps. The expression of these discontents produced some results and a modest programme of modernizing the Gendarmerie was introduced, including for the first time machinery for the voicing of collective grievances, the *commissions de participation.* The malaise of the Gendarmerie in 1989 broke a long tradition of discipline and silence on political matters. The Gendarmerie had, until this point, taken very seriously Art. 78 of the law of 1903 which states: 'The Gendarmerie is expressly required not to interfere in political matters in any

46. This is one of the few police unions affiliated to a national trade union federation, in this case the former Christian Federation which has become close to elements of the Socialist Party.
47. Guyomarch, A., 'Problems of Law and Order in France in the 1980s: Politics and Professionalism', *Police and Society*, 1991, no. 4, 319-332.
48. *Le Monde*, 25/26 December 1988.
49. Reported in *Le Monde*, same date as under 48 supra.

circumstances.' In retrospect 1989 may be seen as an important step on a road to the civilianization of the Gendarmerie but this will take many years, if it happens at all.

Three themes have been emphasized by the FASP and its constituent syndicats in the late 1980s and early 1990s which seem to suggest that many rank-and-file Police have a political outlook which is mildly reformist and open to change. It is difficult, of course, to know whether these express the real aspirations of FASP members or indeed serious commitments by the leadership. The first is the need to re-define the role of the Police to make it 'a real public service' rather than an instrument of repression and control. The second is to simplify the structure of the police by dividing the Police into two categories – an executive corps, and a management and leadership corps. The third is that all Police structures ought to be reviewed and reformed in the light of the new situation which will exist in the European Community in 1993. The adoption of the third theme by the Police unions serves, at the very least, an important educational function in making members aware of the changing European environment.

V. Police-Government Relations

One basic feature of police organization in France dominates the interface between the government and the police – both the Police and the Gendarmerie are under the direct hierarchical control of ministers. This has the side effect of producing a regular stream of politico-police scandals. These affect the Police more often than the Gendarmerie because the military discipline of the latter and their rural base of operations has afforded them some protection. These scandals may be divided into four types: allegations made by journalists and political opponents that ministers have given the Police secret and improper orders; the protection given by senior officials for Police officers which is then abused by those officers; allegations by Police officers accused of offences that they were committed as a result of doing ministers' bidding; allegations that illegal actions by individual Police officers have been encouraged by the government's general policy. The majority of politico-police scandals remain at the level of allegations because the truth is never established.

An example of the first kind cost a senior police officer, the director of the Service Technique de Coopération Internationale de Police (STCIP), his job in 1987 (he was subsequently given a senior position in another service). A passport was issued to a man called Chalier, who was directly implicated in misappropriation of government funds destined for overseas development, in order to allow him to escape to Brazil. This passport was traced back to Delebois, the director of the STCIP, who was promptly arrested. Since Delebois had no obvious motive it was assumed that he had issued the passport on the direct instructions of the Gaullist Minister of the Interior, Charles Pasqua, as part of a complicated manoeuvre to discredit the Socialists in a pre-electoral period. When Pasqua was challenged in parliament, he refused to answer questions on the grounds that this would damage state security (Secret-Défense).

It would be a serious misrepresentation of the police to suggest that they invariably, or even frequently, take illegal instructions from politicians. There are many cases of investigations of corruption at the local level which have involved elected politicians where the police have proceeded without being inhibited by the political consequences, although the more established the politician the more circumspect they tend to be; the celebrated former longtime mayor and deputy of Nice, Jean Medecin, who fled the country in 1990, is a case of police and judicial diffidence but in this case corruption had been a feature of the political machine headed by Medecin and corruption had penetrated deeply into the local society; until the tax authorities started a detailed enquiry into Medecin's personal finances, it was difficult for the police to find reliable sources of information. There are cases, however, where police investigations have rocked the whole of the political establishment. One investigation started by two inspecteurs of the Marseilles fraud squad, Gaudino and Mayot, concerning false receipts revealed the whole illegal system of financing political parties, including the financing of the successful campaign by the Socialists for the presidential and parliamentary elections of 1988 and 1989. This resulted in two presidential amnesties for those who had contravened the law and continuing political embarrassment for President Mitterrand and the Socialist party.[50] Gaudino was subsequently sacked from the Police by the Minister of the Interior for 'not respecting the obligation to behave in a reserved manner' and for 'violation of professional secrecy'.[51]

A remarkably large arms traffic between the Lebanon and France, uncovered in 1990, could not have been conducted by the main instigator without high administrative or political protection. Police sergeant Labourdette was attached to the French embassy in Beirut for the unusually long period of five years and was decorated with the prestigious

50. Gaudino, A., *L'Enqete impossible*, Paris: Albin Michel, 1990.
51. *Le Monde*, 30 March 1991.

Medal of the Ministry of Foreign Affairs for outstanding work in this posting. However, it was revealed in July 1990 that Labourdette had been leader of a ring of between three and five policemen in Beirut, involving about twice that number of their colleagues stationed in France, together with an uncertain number of other persons, in purchasing and sending arms back to France. By the beginning of August the enquiry had seized three rocket launchers, fifteen automatic rifles, eight sub-machine guns, sixty hand guns, four guns with pump action, three grenades and nearly ten thousand cartridges. Other weapons were known to have found their way to criminal milieux in the South of France and have been used against the police in the course of armed robberies. Although there was no direct ministerial involvement in this affair, it caused considerable embarrassment to the Ministry of Foreign Affairs and to the Ministry of the Interior.

Sometimes delinquent police officers use the close relations between the police and politicians to try to camouflage their responsibility for criminal acts. This seems to be the case for the kidnapping and murder of a homosexual protestant minister, pastor Doucé in July 1990. Three officers of the Renseignements Généraux were arrested for this crime and one of them alleged that he had been charged with procuring boys and young men for Socialist politicians and members of the state television service.[52] Whilst such allegations are often dismissed as malevolent attempts to muddy the waters of an investigation, they leave a residue of doubt and suspicion.

Almost any police scandal in France has political implications even when it involves the delinquent act of a single police officer. The shooting dead by Gilles Burgos, a CRS officer of Löic, Lefèvre in the Rue Mogador in Paris on 4 July 1986 is an example. Lefèvre was shot in the back and was not apparently offering any physical threat to Burgos. This happened shortly after the new Right wing Prime Minister Jacques Chirac said that in cases of errors in the course of their duties he would 'cover' police officers. After the shooting it was alleged that the Public Prosecutor's Office, the Police hierarchy and the prefectoral and ministerial authorities did all in their power to protect Burgos.[53] Since 1986 was a record year for the dubious use of firearms by the police, this case

52. *Le Monde*, 2 August 1990.
53. Ancian, J.-M., *La police des polices*, Paris: Balland, 1988, 65-78.

rapidly became a matter of public controversy and the government's general policy on law enforcement was called into question.

VI. Police in the Party Political Debate

Although the experience of the 1980s suggests that police scandals are as likely to occur under governments of the Left as those of the Right, they help to support a typical Right/Left divide on police matters.[54] As in other European countries, there is a tendency in France for Right wing (RPR and UDF) governments to represent themselves as the upholders of law and order and to allege that their opponents are soft on crime and criminals. On his election in 1981, President Mitterrand had the misfortune to order an amnesty of 'political' and other prisoners held either on remand or serving sentences, only to see some of them commit further crimes; these were sometimes of a spectacular nature such as terrorist actions of the founder members of Action Directe, Jean-Marc Rouillan and Nathalie Menignot. The Socialists were also accused of adopting excessively liberal and tolerant attitudes towards certain forms of crime associated with immigrants and marginalized social groups. But there was a general concern about 'insecurity' in the early 1980s and a fear of crime among sections of the community which was not artificially stimulated by politicians seeking votes.

The Socialists tend to accuse their opponents of being long on the rhetoric of law and order, but short on supporting the police and lacking practical ideas about how to make the police more effective and efficient. They go further and allege that the rhetoric of backing the police in rigorous enforcement of the law encourages 'bavures'.[55] There were a series of five such police killings in the first months of the Chirac government in 1986, as well as the beating to death of a student of Algerian parentage in the Latin Quarter during a riot of minor proportions compared with those of 1968 (in which no students were killed).

The anti-immigrant theme and the alleged links between immigrants and criminality was exploited by the extreme Right led by Le Pen and the Front National. This divided the parliamentary Right between those who did not wish to be outbid by Le Pen and those who thought that

54. Guyomarch, A., 'Problems of Law and Order in France in the 1980s: Politics and Professionalism', *Police and Society*, 1991, no. 4, 319-332 for an excellent review of police, law and order issues in the 1980s.

55. Incidents in which the police maltreat or kill suspects or apparently innocent bystanders.

these themes were associated with racism and were, therefore, to be rejected. The FN was also alleged to be an instigator behind the illegal public demonstrations by police officers against the government in 1983 which followed the funerals of police officers killed whilst on duty.

The Socialists have been more inventive than the Right in police policy with the path-breaking Belorgey Report of 1981 which laid the groundwork for subsequent policies for the Police.[56] These policies included measures for crime prevention in 1982-1983 which introduced a multi-agency approach to France for the first time, the 1982 plan of modernization of the police which was slow to get off the ground and had to be re-launched in 1985.[57] Computerization was the symbol of this modernization but it was not until towards the end of the decade that the majority of the police had access to computer facilities and the training to use them. The other aspect of modernization was the provision of in-service training courses, and these are now a general and regular feature of police officers careers. The Socialists did not lose their reforming drive; an important code of police ethics was promulgated in 1986; they have made a further proposal in 1991 for a High Authority for police professional ethics and for the 'transparence' (openness) of police practices; they have also proposed a measure in May 1991, already mentioned, to regulate relations between law enforcement services.[58] These initiatives, together with firm leadership, won for Pierre Joxe, Minister of the Interior until February 1991, admirers within the Police. It remains to be seen what he can achieve as Minister of Defence for the Gendarmerie.

Although ministers, often of governments ostensibly of the Left such as Georges Clemenceau (1906-1909), take considerable care to look after the police, neither they nor their opponents do anything which significantly improves the relations between police and public. One highly respected commentator argues that conflict between police and public is always to the advantage of governments on the grounds that it isolates the police from any sources of political support which could be used to oppose the wishes of the government and the police can be used as the scapegoat for any repressive measures which the government initiates.

56. Belorgey was briefly Director of the National Police before becoming Socialist Deputy for Vichy.
57. See Rouby, P. in: Loubet del Bayle et al., *Police et société*, Toulouse: Presses de l'Institut d'Etudes Politiques de Toulouse, 1988, 131-147 for a local study.
58. Porra, S. and Paoli, C., *Code annoté de déontologie policière*, Paris: Librarie Général de Droit et de Jurisprudence, 1991; they have recently mounted the first timid attempts to decentralize the Police (with pilot studies in five localities to decentralize services to the départements in 1989).

He goes on to argue that public attitudes towards the Police are, in any case, reserved and apprehensive: 'All governments, "red" or "white", royalist or republican, right or left, even though they are inconsistent in other areas, are always faithful to this marvellous method (of maintaining public hostility to the police). The result is in France when a policeman approaches, even if only to ask for a light, one's legs begin to tremble. If a letter arrives from the police station, even if it is to tell you that your wallet has been found, the pulse rate increases. If a policeman enters a compartment where you are deep in converzation with a friend, voices are inevitably lowered.'[59]

Critics and friends of the police are agreed that this general suspicion is a feature of police-public relations in France and that this suspicion is compounded by a widespread lack of knowledge about policing problems. Although both knowledge of policing problems and trust in the Police is improving, these factors weaken the influence the police can exert on legislation and policy.

VII. Police and Terrorism

The general problems of countering terrorism in European countries are well illustrated by the experience of the French police. A centralized police system with close government-police relations should provide a good basis for an anti-terrorism strategy. The French example does not suggest that this is always the case.

In the last two decades, the French government has been confronted with state-sponsored (Iran, Syria, and perhaps the German Democratic Republic), national liberation movement terrorism (Corsican and to a lesser extent Basque and Breton) and radical minority terrorism (Action Directe) as well as terrorists in transit or seeking safe haven (Irish and Italian).[60] France has had a higher incidence than any other European country of bombings, assassinations and kidnapping associated with the Middle East, although a lower incidence of domestically generated terrorist acts than the other major countries of Western Europe.[61] Incidents peaked in the decade from the mid-1970s to the mid-1980s and have ebbed since that time.[62] This decline cannot be attributed to government

59. Casamayor, *La police*, Paris: Gallimard, 1973.
60. Moxon-Browne, E., *Terrorism in France*, London: Institute for Conflict Studies, 1983.
61. Clutterbuck, R., *Terrorism, Drugs and Crime in Europe after 1992*, London: Routledge, 1990.
62. Francis, S.T., 'Terrorist Renaissance: France 1980-1983', *World Affairs*, 1983, 54-58.

policy and police methods, which have often been vacillating and compromising.

There have been various general historical influences operating in the French context – violent overthrow of regimes has been a part of French political history over the last two centuries and the French take a less censorious view of those who are involved in this activity than, for example, the British.[63] Distinguished French politicians have found the need for seeking asylum in other countries and there is a reluctance to infringe rights of asylum leading to the long delay in ratifying the European Convention on the Suppression of Terrorism – only approved after attaching to the instrument of ratification a firmly worded assurance that the right of asylum would not be infringed by the Convention. In addition, uncertainty about general policy objectives, conflicting domestic and international pressures on government and police, a determination to retain flexibility in confronting various kinds of terrorist incident, and a police organization which has not adapted quickly or well to terrorism have been suggested as explanations of French eccentricities in counter-terrorist policy.

Successive French governments have, to some extent unwittingly, created conditions for terrorism to flourish.[64] In the early and mid 1980s, the priorities of French Middle Eastern policy were obscure and, for some, provocative – the willingness to commit troops to 'peace-keeping'in the Lebanon until driven out by terrorist attacks, to supply arms to Iraq and to cultivate Saddam Hussein, to normalize relations with Iran after coming under pressure from terrorist attacks in France, whilst retaining strong links and sympathies with Israel, all created conditions for a complicated relationship between France and the region. It required a change in French foreign policy to extricate France from a cycle of assassinations, kidnapping and apparent attempts to negotiate with terrorist groups. This period seemed to come to an end with the amnesty of the last major Iranian assassin in a French prison, Anis Naccache, in July 1990. The treatment until 1985 of many Spanish Basques fleeing across the Pyrenean frontier as bona fide political refugees and allegedly similar treatment of members of the Italian Red Brigades and its offshoots, responsible for many terrorist attacks, including the assassination of the ex-Prime Minister Aldo Moro, caused serious tension between France and her southern neighbours. Franco-German anti-terrorist cooperation over the 'alliance' between Action Directe and the

63. Casamayor, *Et pour finir le terrorisme*, London: Gallimard, 1983.
64. Anderson, M., *Policing the World; Interpol and the Politics of International Police Co-operation*, Oxford: Clarendon Press, 1989.

Red Army Fraction as well as over Middle Eastern terrorism has, for the most part been good, but France has had difficulty in maintaining its credentials as a reliable partner in other Western capitals.

This was particularly the case under the Right wing government from 1986 to 1988 of Jacques Chirac – despite bold words from its colourful Minister of the Interior, Charles Pasqua, about 'terrorising the terrorists', and ratifying the 1977 European Convention on the Suppression of Terrorism (which it did in 1987). It also passed the anti-terrorist law of September 1986 which *inter alia* allowed for terrorist trials without juries.[65] But it was soon moving away from this apparently hard-line position – refusing to back British and American retaliatory action against Libya and Syria for involvement in terrorist acts, negotiating with the Iranians for the return of hostages, bringing pressure to bear on the judicial process to get a light sentence on a Lebanese in order to put a stop to a wave of terrorist bombings in Paris and suggesting that the Israelis were responsible for an attempt to blow up an El Al airliner at Heathrow. It is against this background that the somewhat confused police response to terrorism must be placed.

French police organization was not set up with anti-terrorist action in mind and it is not especially well-adapted to it. Too many agencies, because of the 'high policing' tradition, are involved: the Direction Générale de la Sécurité Extérieure (DGSE), attached to the Ministry of Defence, whose reputation was low from the 1960s partly because of the involvement of one of its agents in the disappearance of the Moroccan opposition leader Ben Barka from the streets of Paris.[66] Its reputation was further tarnished in the 1980s by a botched car bomb episode in Beirut and the blowing up of the Greenpeace vessel, the Rainbow Warrior, in Auckland Harbour and the subsequent arrest of two of its agents by the New Zealand police[67]; the Direction de la Surveillance du Territoire (DST) is part of the Police and has a major responsibility for counter-espionage and a significant role in counter-terrorism, acting as the lead agency in attempting to counter the 1986 Lebanese bombing campaign in Paris; the General Intelligence Division of the Police, Renseignements Généraux, whose wide terms of reference are to provide the government with information on political, economic and social af-

65. Moxon-Browne, E., 'Terrorism in France', in: Logde, J., ed., *The Threat of Terrorism*, Brighton: Weatsheaf, 1988.
66. Faligot, R. and Krop, P., *La piscine, The French secret service since 1944*, Oxford: Blackwell, 1989.
67. Derogy, J. and Pontaut, J.-M., *Enquete sur trois secrets d'Etat*, Paris: Robert Lafont, 1986, 141-311; Faligot, R. and Krop, P., *La piscine; The French secret service since 1944*, Oxford: Blackwell, 1989, 288-296.

fairs, gathers information, sometimes using illegal telephone tapping, on extremist groups and had a notable success in dismantling the Lyons branch of Action Directe in 1986; the Police Judiciaire acting on the instructions of a juge d'instruction is usually involved when terrorists are being investigated with a view to prosecution; and finally there is the Gendarmerie's elite anti-terrorist squad, trained for commando-type actions against terrorists, the Groupement d'Intervention de la Gendarmerie Nationale (GIGN), founded in 1974. After being made responsible for the protection of the President in 1981, the GIGN suffered a serious loss of reputation in the affair of the 'Irish of Vincennes' when it was accused of acting without legal authority and acting to pervert the cause of justice. The legal actions arising from this affair are still continuing in 1991.

In order to get these competing groups to work together and to ensure proper circulation of information between Intelligence, Police and Gendarmerie, a coordinating committee, Unité de Coordination pour la Lutte Anti-Terroriste (UCLAT), was set up in 1984 under an experienced and strong-minded policeman. This was necessary because the poisonously poor relations between these various agencies and the civil servants trying to coordinate them in the early 1980s has been graphically described by a former head of the DGSE.[68] It apparently remained the case that the Intelligence Services refused to hand over to the Police Judiciaire, important information they had in their possession.[69]

French anti-terrorist action has become more consistent since the re-election of President Mitterrand in 1988. During this election campaign Chirac tried to manipulate the release of French hostages in the Lebanon to his advantage. Mitterrand, despite criticisms of his role during the Greenpeace affair and his controversial amnesty of the Iranian Naccache in 1990, has maintained a firm stance on terrorism for good foreign policy reasons. Disharmony within European Political Cooperation over a relatively peripheral issue such as terrorism could work to the disadvantage of France; European pressure has done much to steady French policy. The arrangements put in place by TREVI for rapid and secure transmission of terrorist related information and the coordination of responses to terrorism by the group have also been influential. The exchange of anti-terrorist liaison officers with the Bundeskriminalamt as a result of the 'secret' 1987 agreement between the Ministers of the Interior, Pasqua and Zimmerman and a more repressive policy concern-

68. Marion, P., *La mission impossible; A la tete des services secrets*, Paris: Calmann-Lévy, 1990.
69. Plenel, E., 'Police et terrorisme', *Esprit*, 1986, 7-20.

ing Basque and Italian fugitives since the middle 1980s has achieved progress at the bilateral level with Spain and Italy.[70] The French improved the rather poor bilateral relations with the British with their success in capturing the Eksund, the vessel running guns from Libya to the IRA. There have been improvements in police arrangements and practices which leave less room for international criticism. In general their has been a revival in the reputation of France in foreign agencies concerned with counter-terrorism.

VIII. Measures to Combat Drug Trafficking and Money Laundering

These areas especially involve international cooperation and, in common with other countries, adapting legislation and police organization to the requirements of international cooperation has been difficult.

Specialized police action against drug trafficking has a longer history in France than in the United Kingdom and the 'brigade des stups' (the drug squad) was set up in the inter-war period. The French Police have also a long experience of operational cooperation with other police forces. The 'French connection' – the traffic in opium from Turkey, refined into heroin in Marseilles and re-exported to the United States – resulted in the 1971 agreement between the United States and France. This has been renewed at five year intervals since and in 1986 Italy and Canada were brought into the agreement. In the original 1971 agreement, three officials from the American Bureau of Narcotics (now the Drug Enforcement Administration) were stationed in Paris and three in Marseilles whilst two officers from the Police Judiciaire were posted to New York. There was provision for the increase in these numbers if necessary and these liaison officers were guaranteed direct access to the most senior levels of the police agencies to which they were attached. According to Art. 7 of the agreement both the French and the American police officers are accredited to participate in investigations (although without police powers) in each others' countries. This agreement has survived despite Marseilles ceasing to be an important centre for refining heroin. Drug abuse has risen sharply since 1971 and DEA officials now give more general help to their French colleagues than the other way round. This agreement has been influential as a model for other

70. *Le Monde*, 10 April 1987.

agreements through which the United States has sought reciprocal help from other countries in suppressing drug-trafficking.

There has been little of the social acceptance of drug taking in France found in the Netherlands in the recent past or in some large cities in Spain in the immediate post Franco period. This has been one of the sources of tension between the French police and immigrant groups – amongst North Africans hashish smoking has been commonplace and trafficking in opium and heroin has been entrenched in the Vietnamese and Chinese communities. The French police have been vigorous and relatively consistent in investigating drug trafficking, although it has been somewhat inhibited when drug taking has penetrated intellectual and artistic milieu (the prosecution of Françoise Sagan is a celebrated example). The courts have taken a repressive view and draconian sanctions are applied to any premises which have been used for trafficking. As has commonly been the case in other countries these repressive measures have mainly picked up the small traffickers – the retailers rather than the wholesalers of drugs. Until effective measures could be enforced for money tracking, investigating and seizing the profits of trafficking, the large dealers could escape unscathed. The array of interests defending banking and commercial secrecy have delayed the introduction of effective measures until 1990.[71]

Another persistent problem has been overlapping competences between police agencies and administrative authorities. It took a long time (four years) to put in place a coordinated system to combat money laundering; a bill was eventually agreed in the Council of Ministers on 9 May 1990, after a long conflict between the Ministries of Finance and Interior over the division of competences between the Police, Customs and financial Civil Servants. In November 1988 Pierre Joxe, the Minister of the Interior, announced the creation of an Office Central de Répression contre la Délinquance Financière (OCRGDF) but the establishment of this office required the signature of the Minister of Finance who refused to agree. There was a conflict about how to deal with the money laundering problem with the Ministry of Finance taking the view that the kind of money tracking which had traditionally been done by customs officers, tax inspectors and treasury officials (all of whom came under its authority) should take the lead whereas the Ministry of the Interior considered that the lead was properly vested in criminal investigators and the investigating magistrates. After the meeting of the Group of 7 in July 1989 at which a number of countries had opposed too

71. *Le Monde*, 10 May 1990.

great a role for the police in financial investigations, President Mitterrand decided that the lead should be taken by the financial services of the state whether the investigation concerned criminal profits from drugs and prostitution or gains from tax fraud. The Ministry of Finance was concerned to preserve as far as possible commercial and banking secrecy and, surprising to a foreign observer, kept the traditional anonymity for purchasers of gold and treasury bonds. The Ministry tried unsuccessfully to extend the criminal investigating powers of Customs, reviving once again the traditional animosity between Police and Customs.

The response of the Ministry of Finance to OCRGDF was the setting up of a specialized 'cell', the Traitement du Renseignement et de l'Action Contre les Circuits Financiers Clandestins (TRACFIN) composed of Customs officials and tax inspectors. This office could block a financial transactions for twelve hours in order to investigate the provenance of funds. After Council of Ministers approval, the ministry of Finance then agreed to OCRGDF, and a deal was struck that it would handle the criminal aspects of money laundering whilst TRACFIN would deal with financial intelligence. Although a certain exchange of personnel was agreed in order to secure good liaison, the division of responsibilities between the two is far from clear and is likely to produce conflict. Even the mission of the OCRGDF to centralize all the intelligence concerning the financial and economic aspects relating to organized crime may be difficult because of rivalries with other central services of the Police Judiciaire (Organized crime, proxenetism, arms trafficking, general intelligence). In addition, chief commissaire René Wack, the first director of the OCRGDF drew attention to the tendency for dubious funds to be more and more internationalized and a role in this area may bring conflict with the strong international office of the Police Judiciaire. It would be surprising indeed if there were no inter-agency conflicts in the area of money laundering.

In repression of drug trafficking, there has not been, at least since the dismantling of the main Marseilles refining laboratories in the 1970s, the same international hesitation or indeed suspicion as that which characterized French anti-terrorist policy. It is recognized to be a difficult country to police with six open land frontiers with neighbouring countries, an important maritime trade, immigrant populations of ethnic groups prone to drug consumption and to drug trafficking, and long-standing weaknesses in financial policing of commerce and industry which make tracing of funds very difficult. Nonetheless there are few doubts about the political resolve or about the effectiveness and relative incorruptibility of the French police in this area.

IX. The French Contribution to International Police Cooperation

The most important French contribution in recent years has undoubtedly been as the host country for Interpol HQ and for many years its most influential member. The second has been through training, technical assistance and the organizing of conferences through the STCIP. The third, by providing an intellectual and a role model for the police organization in other countries, it has been a source of advice for police techniques and police organization abroad.

France was a major influence in the initiation of Interpol by providing the leading delegation to the 1914 conference in Monaco on international police cooperation which started a process leading to the establishment of the International Criminal Police Commission in Vienna in 1923. The ICPC was taken over by the Nazis at the Anschluss and, after the defeat of Germany in 1945, was re-established in Paris in 1946, gaining its present name of International Criminal Police Organization – Interpol when a new constitution was adopted in 1956. The first four Secretaries-General of the organization were French – the first two were part-time and also held senior positions in the French Police. The key figure in the development of the organization was Jean Nepote who was the loyal deputy for the first two Secretaries-General before being appointed himself to that post in 1963 and holding it for over a decade and a half. He achieved his objectives of establishing Interpol as an almost universally recognized international organization with its own resources and its own purpose built headquarters. His personality strongly marked the management, policies and activities of the organization. French influence was reinforced in other ways. The majority of the headquarter's staff until the 1970s were French, often paid by the French government and they were subject to French law. The 1982 Headquarter's Agreement between the French government and Interpol is the most important legal instrument to which Interpol is a party. It contains a provision for data protection which satisfies French law and the chairman of the supervisory board which can check Interpol files for the infringement of data protection rules is a distinguished French journalist.

With the increasing internationalization of the personnel of the headquarters staff, the return of the USA to active participation in the organization in 1979 and the more widespread concern about the international dimension of crime, French dominance was eventually challenged. There was something of an Anglo-American takeover of the organization in the mid-1980s when Raymond Kendall became Secretary General and John Simpson, head of the US Secret Service became

President. There was some resentment in French police circles about this, resulting in two ineffectual attempts to mount candidates to challenge Raymond Kendall which did not prevent his term of office being renewed in 1990. The French, however, had the satisfaction of the election of a French President of Interpol. Although the organization is no longer, as it once seemed to be, an extension of the French Police, the influence of the host country remains strong.[72]

The other main channel of international influence is the Service Technique de Coopération Internationale de Police (STCIP) set up in 1961 mainly to help the countries in Africa which were gaining their independence from France. The main functions of the STCIP are to provide training facilities, both in France and abroad, to advise on police techniques and equipment and, in special cases, to provide operational support. Most of the activities of STCIP are now covered by formal international agreements. Only about twelve police cadets per year come to France for a full two years period of training; most come for short courses in specialized topics. But the main demand is for French instructors to go abroad; by 1987, STCIP instructors had trained more than 70,000 foreign police officers in their own countries. Permanent offices have been established in twenty five countries (mainly francophone but including Saudi Arabia, Bolivia, Mexico and Indonesia) and these provide a variety of assistance.

The Institut International de Police, founded in 1976 is an influential aspect of the work of the STCIP because it brings to Paris senior officers from a large number of countries for international colloquiums. It holds an annual conference on a general theme – for example, Police, Public Order and the Rights of Man (1981), Technology and Methods of Combatting Terrorism (1983), and Police and Technology (1986). This is an example of the way the Service is growing away from its neo-colonial origins.

The broad outlines of French police organization is relatively easy to explain and it has characteristics attractive to developing countries. Nationally, rather than locally, controlled police forces are essential in many of these countries but having two national forces rather than one is an advantage in countries where coup d'état is a constant temptation. The organization of special units for such matters as riot control, political intelligence, frontier control, as well as the criminal investigation police working under the authority of an examining magistrate, all along the lines of the French police, are features which fit the circumstances

72. Anderson, M., *Policing the World; Interpol and the Politics of International Police Co-operation*, Oxford: Clarendon Press, 1989.

of many developing countries. Although the American and British models of police organization are also important in developing countries, they are often seen as too idiosyncratic to be easily adopted.

The international influence of the French police as a leading member of Interpol, as a provider of advice and services, and as a model of policing is likely to remain strong in the foreseeable future.

X. Conclusion

The French police are likely to have direct and indirect influence over the developement of patterns of policing in Europe. Neither the government nor the police can be expected to be as enthusiastic about closer cooperation as their German opposite numbers. But they will certainly try to have two direct inputs. The first will take the form of initiating positive proposals through TREVI, European Political Cooperation and any new Community or inter-governmental fora which emerge from the 1991 inter-governmental conferences concerning closer police cooperation. Second, the French have a pool of experienced senior police officials with the ambition and experience to help organize and manage institutions for closer police cooperation. The indirect effect will simply be by 'being there' – the French have in some respects the oldest and the strongest police tradition of any of the Community partners. Despite all its difficulties and imperfections the French example will be an intellectual and practical presence of considerable weight.

The Belgian Perspective on the Internationalization of Police Cooperation in Western Europe

Lode de Witte

I. European Police Cooperation: A New Danger to Our Democracies ?

Over the last years, European police cooperation has received particular attention. The large number of seminars and the plethora of articles and books on the subject are a clear indication to this. When I read some of these documents, I was almost left with the impression that European police cooperation is a large scale secret international conspiracy. A near mythical dimension is ascribed by some to European police cooperation networks. The Schengen Treaty and the Action Programme of Dublin are considered as steps in a well prepared and systematic approach, the main objectives of which would be to submit Europe as a whole to an uncontrollable police network, and to rule out, or at least to seriously restrict, the individual rights of European citizens. For a number of years I have been following the developments in European police cooperation. The image of European police cooperation as a new danger to our democracies does not strike me as a true interpretation of reality. Therefore I wish to try and put the subject into perspective.

In the first place, I want to emphasize that not all developments in this field are new. For quite some time, police services have been cooperating internationally, either on the basis of bilateral agreements or within the framework of multilateral agencies, such as Interpol. Of course it is true that, during the last decade, quite a few new international groups and committees have been created, but very often their achievements are not nearly as revolutionary as people generally think. Here I would like to quote professor Fijnaut, who examined the terms of the Schengen Treaty and who has reached the conclusion that newly proposed arrangements for international legal cooperation are not in fact different from already existing regulations.[1] However, the fact that the countries concerned have managed to enter into a multilateral convention is a tremendous improvement on the previous situation.

When reading an article by John Evans, I discovered a rather nice argument by Sir Leon Brittan about the control system at the internal borders of the European Community.[2] What will be the difference when internal borders are opened up? Today, as these internal borders still exist, everyone in principle has to be subjected to checks. In practice, however, only a few people are stopped. After the abolition of internal borders, people will in principle no longer have to be checked. But, as an exception to the new rules, some people might in fact still be checked. So, according to Sir Leon, in practice there hardly will be any difference. We Belgians can actually see how this works even now. When we go to the Netherlands, we cross an open border and are not checked. When we go to France or Germany, we cross a real border, but we are never checked. The only difference lies in the fact that, when crossing the German or French border, we have to slow down. At the Belgian-Dutch border we do not even have to do that.

Of course, not everything will remain the same in a different guise. Fortunately there has been real progress and evolution in a number of fields. But discussions on police cooperation are neither inspired by a will to take power, nor are they guided by some perverted desire to submit a Unified Europe to the will of the police. They rather address themselves to the very real concerns of developing criminality and its internationalization, and to the fact that many crimes now go unpunished. Indeed, police forces are in search of an answer to social change. Every day it becomes more obvious that social change not only brings about good things, but also bad ones. People are increasingly mobile, which I think is very good for personal and cultural development. The economy increasingly operates internationally, creating possibilities for more progress and with time also for a better distribution of wealth.

But there are dark sides to this evolution and we have to concern ourselves nowadays with increasing financial fraud, with trafficking of weapons, drugs and waste products, with pickpockets who travel from one country to another and with burglaries committed deliberately across the border. More and more often police officers and politicians

1. Fijnaut, C., 'Naar een Gemeenschappelijke regeling van de politiële samenwerking en de justitiële rechtshulp', in: Fijnaut, C., Stuyck, J. and Wytinck, P., eds., *Schengen: Proeftuin voor de Europese gemeenschap?*, Antwerpen – Arnhem, Kluwer Rechts-wetenschappen – Gouda Quint, 1992, 89 – 117.
2. Evans, J., *Europe after 1992*, Address to the International Association of Chiefs of Police, 31 march 1992.

have to deal with such problems and no country on its own can react appropriately to such international criminal activities. It is when we meet face to face with victims of crime and when we witness enormous material losses and damages, that we feel most painfully our lack of efficiency. Meetings on European police cooperation are characterized by the sincere will to set these things right.

In the third place, I wish to emphasize that international police cooperation has not developed so much in order to serve its own ends, but rather as a necessary contribution towards a better implementation of human rights, which itself depends on the opening up of borders. For too long the European Community has contended mainly for free circulation of capital and for free competition. The fact that, recently, more and more interest has been shown in a Europe of citizens and of human rights for everybody, certainly is a sign of considerable progress. To study, to work and to live in a foreign country is more natural for many young people nowadays than to live in another town in their own country was for youngsters fifty years ago. When this evolution is no longer obstructed by a plethora of restrictive rules and regulations, by bureaucracy and red tape, then real progress will have been made.

European cooperation is a normal and logical step in an ever shrinking world. Since the Second World War, most European countries have experienced similar kinds of evolution. As means of communication get increasingly faster, as people become a lot more mobile, as not only trade but also social and cultural exchanges are organized on an ever wider scale, we see more and more people leaving the security and safety of their own local communities. Of late we also see that they are no longer afraid to leave the 'relative security' of their own country. However, this evolution is taking place inch by inch, step by step. Indeed, even when all these new trends occur, still people are not prepared to give up what they feel to be their own identity. Over and over again, discussions prove the great importance people attach to their own legal system, which meets their own requirements and which expresses their own views on social and criminal problems. In fact, sometimes it even looks like an Echternach procession: each step forward – under the impulse of either hot news about international criminality or of a growing feeling of insecurity – is followed by a step backward – caused by backslides inevitable in every kind of action and by the fact that people do not want to abandon their own values and work styles.

Looking at Belgium once more helps us to understand this process. Here we are witnessing the same kind of ambivalence towards an evolution, which so far remains incomplete. Belgium is indeed characterized by a strong sense of local autonomy, which originated in the Middle

Ages. I think the Belgian situation is quite unique in Europe in that respect. In our country we have a strong local police force, which is paid and organized by the local authorities and which takes its orders from the same even now. Cooperation between these local police forces (as well as cooperation with the national police force) often has been and still is very laborious. The case of the Brussels north station area illustrates this. The Brussels gare du nord is situated on the territory of two municipalities, Brussels being not just one administrative entity, but an agglomeration of 19 municipalities. The gare du nord is situated partly on the territory of Schaerbeek and partly on the territory of Saint-Josse. The delinquency rate and criminality in this area are quite high: partly because of trafficking in trains coming, for example, from the Netherlands and partly because of typical inner city problems. To this day it is very difficult to set up coordinated operations between the police forces of the municipalities involved, Schaerbeek and Saint-Josse. For quite some time, Schaerbeek has been administered by an avowed right wing majority, whereas the mayor of Saint-Josse for the past 40 years has been the popular Left wing Socialist Guy Cudell. Up till now, both local authorities feel reluctant about any type of cooperation between their police forces, as they fear such cooperation may lead to loss of traditional methods and values for their own men. Those who know the political situation may be inclined to sympathize with the position of the authorities concerned, but one still cannot ignore the social cost of the problems which remain unanswered. Criminality in the north station area cannot be dealt with efficiently, as long as each municipal police force continues to work on its own. Every day people come and complain about the high delinquency rate and about the obvious lack of security in the north station area.

This is a clear cut example, but it is typical of a number of situations. Therefore, as Belgians, on the one hand we can easily understand why people should want their particular characteristics to be preserved and respected, but on the other hand we fully realize that cooperation is a necessity, because we know all too well how much absence of cooperation costs us and how it leads to inefficiency and consequently lack of safety for the population.

So, European police cooperation as such is not a new adventure. For the last few decades, many European countries have been trying to cope with the need for better coordination between their own police forces. Cooperation on a European level means working on an even wider scale. The success of this initiative will depend on the achievement of two important targets: more efficiency in day to day police actions and – at the same time – an open, democratic handling of cases. Both requirements are quite evident, but I think it is good to keep them constantly in mind. It is not without reason that in my country, after years of discussions and thorough parliamentary inquiries, these two objectives have been explicitly put down in the first article of the law introducing the establishment of a parliamentary supervision committee on police work.

II. Attention to Security Problems in Border Areas

When I talk about efficiency of police operations, I am not merely referring to either arrests of members of the Provisional IRA or to the follow up of international trafficking. We need to pay as much attention to what the police can effectively do about growing cross-border criminality and about growing feelings of insecurity in border areas. Although in the newspapers people may read about all kinds of international trafficking, on the whole they still feel more threatened by noticeable increases in petty crimes, which are made easier by the increased possibilities to play off differences between neighbouring countries. Too often, authorities are concerned only with international trafficking, and too often we forget people's concerns and we make our decisions without consulting them. One of the lessons of the discussions on the Maastricht Treaty was that, within the framework of European cooperation, we ought to pay more attention to the actual problems which people face in their daily lives.

I now want to go more deeply into the question of police actions in those border areas which are characterized by close social and economical cooperation. First I want to stress that I do not think that less importance should be attached to the fight against international trafficking and fraud: on a European level, agreements ought to be made in order to discourage and dismantle these networks. If I want to give more thought to the question of the border areas, it is because on the whole little attention is paid to this matter. I would like to give you two examples of border regions which have to cope with a high rate of criminality. I shall treat them both from a Belgian point of view.

The first example concerns the French-Belgian border, in particular the region of Kortrijk, Moeskroen, Lille and Roubaix, on which research has be done by W. Bruggeman, B. De Ruyver and P. Zanders.[3] They came to the conclusion that on the one hand individual cross-border delinquency is on the increase, but remains mainly restricted to

3. Dierkens, R., Bruggeman, W., De Ruyver, B. and Zanders, P., *Grensoverschrijdende criminaliteit*, Gent, Rijksuniversiteit Gent, School voor Criminologie, 1991.

towns close to the border. On the other hand there is semi-professional organized crime, where criminals quickly move along the big connecting roads in order to organize hold-ups on luxury goods shops, even as far away as Gent and Antwerpen. I would like to point out that delinquency in that particular area has social causes and can be explained from a sociological point of view. The North of France has considerable economic difficulties and parts of the population have social problems. The Kortrijk-area on the contrary is known as the 'Belgian Texas'; it is known as a rich area with little unemployment. Unless the social and economic situation in the area of Lille, Roubaix and Tourcoing improves, a high delinquency rate in that part of the country is quite a normal thing to expect, even without a border. However, today's criminals use the border in order to expand their criminal activities. Differences between police structures, legislation and judicial systems are exploited and criminals make their haul on one side of the border and then cross over it to escape detection and prosecution.

During the last few years there has been growing concern over this particular situation. I myself come from that region. I lived there until the second half of the Seventies and until then such problems were unknown. During the last few years, concern has grown among the authorities as well as among the population itself. The abolition of border controls as part of European unification will further increase anxiety in the border region. From research by Prof. B. De Ruyver it appears that about half of the persons whom he questioned about the opening up of the borders expect an increase in criminality. Thus very real problems of increasing criminality and of increasing feelings of insecurity will have to be faced.

The second area which I want to quote as an example is a region which covers three countries: the Aachen area in Germany, combined with the area of Maastricht, Heerlen and Sittard in the Netherlands and the Belgian areas stretching out beyond Eupen and Verviers, on to Liège and to the area of Tongeren-Genk. This region does not have to cope with large socio-economic differences and the consequences resulting from it, as was the case in the first example. Here, there are very close socio-economic interrelations and very heavy cross-border traffic, which inevitably bring about some criminal activities. Again this is worsened by differences in legislation, especially drugs legislation. This is certainly not the right place to discuss which laws on drugs are the more efficient ones, but we cannot help concluding that differences in legislation result in large numbers of Belgians going to the Netherlands for supplies, and this causes problems. It is clear that delinquency will undoubtedly still exist in a politically and legally Unified Europe, but transgressing the law is certainly made easier thanks to remaining divergences in legislation and in police and legal structures.

With these two examples, which appear to be the most important ones for Belgium, but which certainly are not the only ones that can be thought of, I have tried to point out that both the population and the authorities are losing sleep over new forms of criminality encountered by too many in their daily lives. I agree with Prof. C. Fijnaut when he says that these new factors, and the police initiatives to face them, are as important for European unification as are the other forms of international police cooperation, which the politicians of Europe usually deal with.[4]

It is not only natural but also encouraging that during the past few years initiatives have been taken to try and find a solution to the problems caused by cross-border delinquency. A form of cooperation which is known by the somewhat difficult name Nebedeag-Pol has been in place since 1969 in this area where the three countries meet around Meuse and Rhine, following earlier initiatives launched on a bilateral basis. From 1969 onwards each country has established a point of contact (in Aachen, Heerlen and Verviers) where there has been an exchange of police officers in order to improve contacts as well as information about each others' police system. It was further agreed that there should be a regular exchange of investigation documents, daily reports and police journals. During the following years cooperation increased, particularly by the drawing up of a trilingual report file, by the creation of a direct telex connection between Maastricht, Eupen, Verviers and Aachen and by the establishing of permanent radio-contact between a number of police headquarters. Over the years cooperation has grown stronger and stronger. At the end of the 1970s, attempts were made to create a legal arrangement for this kind of cooperation but they all came to nothing. This did not however prevent the police authorities of the three countries from trying to further improve means of cooperation. Over the last few years work has been done on an international alarm system, for use in cases of major crimes. Furthermore a continuous effort has been made to steadily improve information exchanges between all services concerned.

In the French-Belgian border area around Kortrijk, Moeskroen, Lille and Roubaix extensive consultation has taken place to improve cooperation in the fight against criminality. Since 1989, practical training of police officers has been organized and an agreement has been made to

4. Fijnaut, C., 'Tussen misdaadbestrijding en strafrechtspleging: De internationale samenwerking van de politie in West-Europa', *Delikt en Delikwent*, 1990, no. 7, 623-638.

exchange information monthly. Cooperation in this area does not yet have the smooth structure of Nebedeag-Pol, but in the spring of 1992 a conference was organized with, among others, the prefect of the département du Nord, the governor of the province of West-Vlaanderen and the attorney general of Mons. This means we are just at the beginning of a number of further cooperative developments in the region.

III. An Unsound Legal Basis for Cross-border Organization

When some form of cooperation beyond borders is set up, then practical, technical and legal problems are met with, which can only in a number of cases be solved by the authorities directly concerned. A very obvious difficulty lies in the knowledge of each others' language and each others' methods and work organization. In order to set such things right, the relevant authorities themselves can develop a lot of initiatives. However, this does not mean that they do not deserve some support at the national and the European level. In the technical field, difficulties will mainly lie in the compatibility of different communication systems. Up to a certain level this can be solved locally and to a certain extent this has already been done. But further agreements will be required between the countries involved. The same is true for mutual support with very specialized equipment, which has already proved to be very useful in the case of some serious crimes (as in the hostage case in Tilff).

Everybody will readily agree that legal problems are often the toughest ones to resolve. It goes without saying that high technical performance is not the only thing needed for an exchange of information. Indeed, an appropriate legal framework is needed just as much. Which matters are suitable for exchange; in which way can respect for private life be guaranteed; and how can exchanged information be protected? These are essential issues to which no suitable solution can be offered on a local level. Such is even more the case with special police techniques, as controlled missions or undercover operations, both very sensitive topics in our democratic societies. Given the need to respect the human rights and the individual liberties of citizens and the need to have a firm case when taking legal action, making appropriate legal arrangements in those cases where police services and public prosecutor's departments cooperate across borders, is of the utmost importance. It is equally important to ensure that the concerned authorities have sufficient control over cooperation initiatives by the police. As far as Belgium is concerned, where the public prosecutor's department is not only responsible for prosecution but also for investigation, it is obvious that international cooperation agreements for the investigation of crimes should be enforced and executed under the authority and the control of the public prosecutor's department.

Because of differences in criminal legislation, some acts or behaviour are punishable in one country and not in another. Drugs legislation in the Netherlands is an example which is perhaps too frequently quoted. Differences between financial and tax legislation between Luxemburg and its neighbours are in my opinion at least as important. Another example concerns weapons and hunting legislation, where especially France appears to be more lenient. This results in very real problems. For instance, on the North Sea coast, on the French border with Belgium, at Bray-Dunes, hundreds of French hunters wait to shoot migratory birds coming from Belgium. Protected bird species are not spared. These examples make clear that European unification will inevitably require a harmonization of our criminal laws.

Police services can already fall back on a certain number of bilateral agreements providing a legal basis for the establishment of certain arrangements. Some of these agreements are direct arrangements between police services. Immediately after the First World War, the Belgian gendarmerie established conventions with the gendarmerie of France (1919) and Luxembourg (1920). After the Second World War, a similar agreement was made with the Dutch national police forces, establishing rules concerning exchange of information on serious crimes in border areas and on direct contact, when necessary. The Treaty concluded with Germany in 1957 was not only applicable to the gendarmerie, but to all police forces operating in border areas. The latter treaty not only concerns the exchange of information, but also provides for the possibility of sending liaison officers. And it is obvious that general conventions between countries offer better opportunities for cooperation. The best example of this is undoubtedly the Benelux Convention concerning extradition and legal aid in criminal cases. According to its Arts. 26 and 27 this Convention offers the opportunity to cooperate in the field of investigation of crimes, by sending police officials as consultants and by making possible the tracking down of suspects across the border.

It is clear that these conventions and treaties do not so far offer a sufficient legal basis for border area cooperation in trying to cope with cross-border delinquency. Police forces cannot be blamed for the fact that they try to settle daily problems by entering into agreements which, even if not incompatible with the laws, nevertheless are made on a quite inadequate legal basis. Therefore the involvement of competent political and legal authorities may be a safeguard against possible actions just on their own behalf. In any case, it should be obvious by now that this ambiguous situation needs to be straightened out.

This is the reason why I fully agree with the arguments in favour of clear legal arrangements.[5] These arrangements will give police forces the opportunity to cooperate no longer on an unofficial, but on an official basis. They will be able to enter into agreements based on formal legal rules and to set up open modes of operation. This means that it will be easier to define responsibilities for the authorities who are directly in charge of police cooperation. Herefore I plead for international discussions which focus not only on cooperation between national police forces, but also on the creation of a legal framework, in which 'grass-root' cooperation can then be activated. We should not build castles in the air, but make it clear that, by means of international cooperation, we want to create opportunities which de facto enable us to tackle the very real problems of the people who live in the border areas.

I think the Schengen Convention gives police forces the opportunity to go into actual cooperation arrangements, such as exchange of information, contacts, hot pursuit and cross-border observation. I think that criticism about the fact that too few people were involved in the conclusion of the Schengen Convention is very correct and that in future methods must indeed be elaborated to guarantee sufficient democratic control. Such control is especially needed over the discussions in the Executive Committee and over the decisions made by it. No matter how, I think the best thing to do is to implement the Schengen Convention as soon as possible, in the form in which it was concluded, but with the very clear understanding that certain preconditions must be fulfilled. By this I mean that the Convention should not come into effect in Belgium until the moment when we have an official act on the protection of privacy, that is to say clear guidelines for the creation and for the treatment of data banks. Both such an act on the protection of privacy and the Schengen Convention are subjects of parliamentary discussions for the moment and both should be approved by the end of this year. This means they could come into effect on January 1, 1993.

As to Schengen, it is true that it does not offer one and the same solution to the problem of cross-border pursuit. There is a choice between different options, not only in the field of the distance which police forces may cover on another country's territory, but also as far as duration of pursuit, possibilities to arrest, and the kind of crimes that lead to pursuit are concerned. However, I do not see problems be-

5. Bruggeman, W., 'De internationale politiële samenwerking', in: D' Haenens, J. and De Ruyver, B., eds., *Schengen en de praktijk*, Gent: Mys en Breesch, 1992, 85-96.

cause of the possibility to chose in these matters: I do not think that international conventions should lead to exactly the same solutions for all kinds of problems between all countries. It is first of all important to create an adequate legal framework leading to agreements with a formal legal basis. Secondly, I really do not mind, on the contrary, if actual agreements differ and if specific situations and susceptibilities are taken into account. I do not think our aim is to create a Europe that is identical everywhere. The challenge which we should take up, is to try and give a clear and feasible answer to problems related to cross-border delinquency originating from the planned abolition of border control from 1993 onwards.

I plead for greater attention to cross-border cooperation and this requires that police officers and services involved in the matter participate in the discussions on police cooperation. This means that each country should create advisory committees of police officers, such as the International Advisory Committee in Great Britain, created by the Association of Chief Police Officers and the Advisory Committee set up in the framework of the Dutch CRI. In countries such as Belgium, characterized by the existence of different police forces, those committees will, of course, have to be composed of people belonging to the different police services. The fact that the TREVI groups are already not only composed of civil servants but also of police officers offers better opportunities to mention as well as try and find a solution to actual police problems.

IV. European Decision-making Must Become More Transparent

My first message was that international debates about police cooperation should increasingly focus on the problems of people living in border areas. In this framework I already came up in defence of openness and clear arrangements. Now I want to fully take up this case. First of all, I think it is the lesson we have to derive from the public debate on the Maastricht Treaty, the way it was held in different countries. The European decision-making process is too complicated, insufficiently transparent, spread over a plethora of groups and committees, and forms a knot which even specialists distangle with great difficulties. There is an overpowering feeling that bureaucrats have long discussions, but nobody knows either the real subject of these discussions, or their link with other meetings in other committees, with other civil servants.

I do not have the intention to present another general survey of the existing international cooperation agencies on police, security and criminality. Everybody undoubtedly already had the opportunity to examine thick dissertations and research reports, in which such surveys were published. The reader of this article will know, although perhaps only by name, most of the cooperation agencies, created either within the framework of the United Nations, the Council of Europe, the European Community or in another multilateral frameworks. The impressive number of pages necessary, over and over again, to explain objectives, composition, mission and functioning of these agencies shows the enormous overlapping there must be. 1993 is the right moment for the European countries to proceed to a radical reduction of this plethora of agencies.

Of course, this does not mean that all overlapping can be avoided. Let me give an example. The Pompidou Group, active on the level of the Council of Europe, tried to set up a multidisciplinary approach to the drugs problem, involving at the same time foreign policy (development cooperation and external trade, in order to promote drug substituting crops), as well as the discouraging of drug abuse (with a tremendous role for schools), investigation and prosecution of drug trafficking, medical and therapeutical crisis centres for drug addicts and other aspects of drug addiction. A good drugs policy is subordinated to the creation of a multidisciplinary forum, because of the need to start off from a coordinated and integrated approach to the problem. TREVI group III, on the other hand, debates about drugs from a police point of view. The advantage of TREVI is that drug investigations can be treated in connection with other police subjects. Each police constable and each police officer know that, nowadays, drugs are not an isolated problem, but are related to racketeering, to fraud, to money laundering. So, from a police point of view, it is necessary to discuss drugs in connexion with other crimes.

Simplifying will not be an easy task. Either the Pompidou Group is abolished, and there is no longer a multidisciplinary forum to discuss approaches to the drugs problem. Or we decide that TREVI should no longer deal with drugs problems, and policemen will lack information on the connections between differents kinds of trafficking. You could even decide to join the activities of both groups, but, in that case, the plethora of subgroups and the amalgam of problems would certainly lead to inefficiency. The best solution is that we admit the fact that there always will be some kind of overlapping. But even in the case that some overlaps are inevitable, this does not mean that radical steps to simplification are either impossible or unnecessary. All our credibility will be lost if we do not succeed in clearing up the patchwork of debates and cooperations.

I will not try to determine here which groups have to be maintained and which ones should be reformed or abolished. I only want to repeat that January 1, 1993, is the ideal moment to start with a thorough reflection at a European level on what police cooperation should be about. Simplification would of course be ideal if one simple structure for all police cooperation were established – at least as far as the Twelve are concerned. Thanks to a thorough simplification of the structures of police cooperation, more efficiency could be guaranteed and democratic control from the outside would be easier. The goodwill of those who deliberate in European fora on police cooperation cannot be questioned here but their good intentions are not sufficient and do not give them the right to uncontrolled authority in these deliberations. The police itself, the population in border areas, the authorities on local and national levels, as well as the people's representatives in the national and the European Parliament, are convinced that a better police cooperation is necessary if one wants to cope with cross-border criminality. Still this does not allow us to have such cooperation started without a proper democratic and judicial control. I deliberately mentioned the European Parliament, as it is well known that within this institution critical remarks on the way police cooperation is now organized have often been uttered. However, this does not mean that the European Parliament is as such ill-disposed toward police cooperation on a European level. Critical remarks more often refer to the way in which this cooperation is realized today and to the absence of sufficient control mechanisms on cross-border activities.

Thus simplifying is the first condition to openness and to supervision, both essential for democracy. But more is needed and European police cooperation ought to be embedded in a normal democratic and judicial structure. Police forces sometimes are inclined to look upon themselves as instruments only to be controlled by the executive. In democratic countries it is essential that not only the results of each crime investigation but more specifically the way in which evidence has been obtained can be judicially supervised. Parliaments should have the real possibility to control the entire functioning of police services. If in the end we want to have a democratic Europe, then European police cooperation cannot back out of these two requirements.

The Schengen Convention needs the approval of the national parliaments and the debates of the last two years prove that this is not a pure formality. Nevertheless, it would have been much better if a lot more openness had been shown during the preparation of the Schengen Convention and if different countries had, at an earlier stage, the possibility to discuss the contents of that Convention in a democratic way. Europol is considered in the Maastricht Treaty as an intergovernmental matter and TREVI Ministers have fortunately decided in Lissabon that Europol should get a basis in accordance with international law. This implies that the Europol Treaty will need the approval of the national parliaments. Hopefully, discussions on the mission and on the competences of Europol will be open in the preparatory phase and not only at a later stage, as has been the case with the Schengen Convention. As it is an agreement and consequently a compromise between different partners, each project of a treaty offers the disadvantage that it can only be approved or rejected by a national parliament but that its terms cannot be modified unilaterally by a parliament. Therefore proposals or objections against some terms must already be put forward during the negotiation phase.

The Schengen Convention and Europol Treaty will be of the utmost importance in determining the future scope of police actions and the legal position of citizens. Chances to claim the necessary information and control are still open to the national parliaments and they should be taken. In my opinion, it would have been much better if in the Maastricht Treaty police cooperation had been considered as a Community matter, and not as an intergovernmental one. European Community action rules could then have been applied. I feel the Maastricht Treaty does not go far enough here. This point of view is shared by the Belgian government as a whole. If European police cooperation would have been a Community matter, the European Parliament would have had a much larger role in controlling it and the European Court of Justice would have become competent on arguments concerning these matters.

If I believe that democratic control by the European Parliament is absolutely necessary, I still think this by itself is not sufficient. Police action is so strictly linked with the sovereignty of a state and with the individual rights and liberties of citizens, that I think supervision by the national parliaments should also be guaranteed. Even with a large involvement by the European Parliament, I would hardly be satisfied with a concept for police cooperation on a European level without appropriate control and approvals by the national parliaments as an inbuilt safeguard. The intention of the European Commission to involve national states and national parliaments in the preparation of its directives, seems to me a step in the right direction. As far as police cooperation is concerned, extra guarantees for supervision by the European Parliament and the national parliaments seem to be necessary. However, since police cooperation is not a Community matter, these questions are not yet the order of the day. I very much regret this and I consider it as a democratic failing which we have to cope with, by trying to organize a debate on police cooperation in the national parliaments.

In a democratic society, politics is nothing without police and vice versa. Politics without police would mean that authorities are powerless and thus that society is powerless against individual excesses and against criminals pursuing their own interests and power. A powerless state can never survive as a democracy. Police without politics would mean that police services are able to judge for themselves what to do and what not to do, that they are not controlled by democratically elected representatives. Politics and police are tied together. In the world of tomorrow, a European society and a politically unified Europe are not imaginable without European police cooperation. European police cooperation cannot be made acceptable without political authority and without supervision by parliament and justice.

The Dutch Perspective on the Internationalization of Police Cooperation in Western Europe

Jan Peek and Merle Hoefman

I. Introduction

The title of our address, as you can see from your programme, is 'The Dutch perspective on the internationalization of police cooperation in Western Europe'. To our mind the internationalization of the police should be dealt with from two angles, namely: the internationalization of police work and the internationalization of police organization.

The Netherlands goes on the assumption that organizational aspects are geared to practical aspects. In other words, the organizational arrangements follow on from what is required of the work and not vice versa. True to this point of departure, we shall first look at the internationalization of police work and we shall then go on to deal with the internationalization of police organization.

II. Internationalization of Police Work

There is no need for us to tell the police officials and others present in the audience here about how much crime has crossed frontiers. Previous speakers have already gone into this in detail and have already provided enough interesting material for today. So, the phenomenon of cross-border crime is not new. After all, talks on international cooperation to suppress crime were started as early as the nineteenth century.

Meanwhile, the whole of social life has become permeated by international aspects. The international cooperation and integration movement, and more specifically the European one, has many actors: governments, industries, banking institutions, universities, etc. More and more people and aspects of society are becoming involved. They all play their role and the input of all is decisive for the results. But we should realize that no matter how important the role of governments may be in this regard they do not create Europe! The basis is laid by technical, financial and market developments, by societies' structures and the extent to which people want to make use of these. Governments function within that ambit. They do not create the future but their task is to stimulate by taking initiatives, by creating conditions, by meeting basic requirements and by creating the juridical structure that lives up to the demands of democracy and legal and legitimate principles. Crime is local where social and economic life is locally oriented. Where social and economic traffic is internationally oriented, crime is equally so.

For the police this means that nationally they have to be placed in a position to cope with the work that is arising through internationalization, both in terms of people, resources and powers. We should like to look briefly at these three aspects.

First of all people: we have people, but not enough, as many a police chief will tell you. In any event they have to be equipped for their work in an international context. Considerable effort will have to be made, especially in the field of training. Key aspects here are: knowledge of foreign languages and specialist jargon, knowledge of foreign legal systems and enforcement structures, social and practical skills and skills in dealing with people from different cultures ('know your neighbour', and we would add, 'respect your neighbour', the slogan of many a study conference at the German police training institute, Gimborn), the creation of a network of contacts and the like.

As regards resources let us say the following: naturally there is an ongoing need for sufficient ready cash to pay for all the work that is being done as part of the internationalization of police work (travel expenses, translation costs). It would be going too far to go into all this at the present juncture. But there are other aspects which spring to mind when one speaks of resources in this connection, and these are, above all, in the domain of technology. For example, means of communication. In frontier border zones there is a need for direct communication between incident rooms. Observation teams are requiring new facilities in connection with their operations far beyond the home country borders. In incidental cases (for example kidnapping) the way the communication problem is dealt with can be done on a more ad hoc basis. Other resources which one can think of in this connection are teaching aids and information carriers (libraries, documentation centres, thesauruses, course ware and hard and software).

That brings us lastly to powers: powers for the purpose of international cooperation in carrying out police tasks have been regulated up to now in Dutch legislation in two ways:

- In legislation laying down the power to enter into international cooperation (sections 552 ff. of the Dutch code of criminal procedure);

- Through the internationalization of criminal law, whereby acts perpetrated abroad fall within the ambit of Dutch criminal law.

Another way of improving international cooperation and regulating powers in this connection is to make international agreements on the subject and to lay these down in conventions.

The first forum in which this took place was the Council of Europe. The result was two important conventions namely the European Convention on Extradition (of 13 December 1957) and the European Convention on Mutual Legal Assistance in Criminal Matters (of 20 April 1959), both later extended by the addition of Protocols.

Another important international stimulus with a far-reaching influence on powers regarding police work is the European Convention for the Protection of Human Rights and Fundamental Freedoms of 4 November 1950 and other results of activities within the Council of Europe, such as those relating to data protection (1981 Data Protection Convention and Recommendation R (87) 15 of the Committee of Ministers of the Council of 17 September 1987 regarding police files). These latter have given a completely new profile within police work to the rights of suspects and the openings available to legal counsel as well as the rights of citizens with regard to personal records.

The Schengen Agreement of 14 June 1985 stipulates that a new European society in which states, while keeping their sovereignty, abandon their frontier demarcations and border checks, requires further arrangements for the police and security. After five years of intensive discussion the ideas on this have been encapsulated in the Convention to implement the Schengen Agreement (19 June 1990) and above all in Title III, police cooperation, the cooperation of the judicial authorities and cooperation on special topics such as combatting illegal drug trafficking and illegal possession of fire arms and munition.

Two items strike one when examining this Convention:

- The connection between the improvement in police cooperation and the improvement in cooperation between judicial authorities;
- The low level of institutionalization, which is connected with the fact that the Schengen partners wished to be a fore-runner for the Twelve. They proceeded on the principle that the results of their discussions should serve within the broader context of the Twelve and that any endeavours or principles within that framework should not be frustrated.

In drawing up the Convention the partners did their utmost to avoid rediscovering the wheel. Wherever possible, existing arrangements and conventions have been latched on to. An interesting conclusion which one was forced to draw seeing the evolution of the Convention was that there was no international law ruling to which reference could be made for international police cooperation.

The governments have signed the Convention and increasingly the various parliaments are judging it warranted to give their approval (France, Luxembourg, Spain). In the Netherlands in June 1992, after extensive debate the Lower House of Parliament gave its consent with a convincing majority of 120 of the 150 votes cast. Otherwise, the sections on the police and the judicial authorities generally met with agreement in the parliamentary debates. From this it emerges that the Convention has been accepted as a balanced and politically and legally warranted document. The Schengen Convention can thus be judged to be the first instrument of international law which involves far-reaching international police cooperation within a sound political and legal framework. We should like to refer to three examples of powers which have been laid down in the Schengen Convention.

First of all powers in the field of information exchange.

Art. 39 of the Convention deals with the exchange of information upon request, for the benefit of preventing and investigating criminal acts. To be clear, let it be said that this power is not a substitute for judicial legal assistance. It only applies in so far as the making or dealing with the request, under national law, is not the preserve of the judicial authorities and no coercion need be applied to comply with the request.

Art. 46 of the Convention offers the possibility of providing information, without any prior request, which may be important to the recipient partner in giving assistance for the suppression and prevention of future criminal acts or ensuring that public order and security are not jeopardised. Needless to say, a strict ruling has been included in the Schengen Convention for the types of information exchange involved to protect personal privacy and data.

The other two examples of powers which are regulated in the Convention which we should like to refer to here are the power to carry out cross-border surveillance and the power to carry out cross-border hot pursuit. If there is one subject which is politically and socially sensitive in practice then it is the presence of foreign police officials on alien territory. Every police official and citizen senses that in such cases individual sovereignty is touched at the core. It was accepted that, with the disappearance of frontiers, these two instruments were indispensable. However the more police action became openly manifest in exercising the powers in question, the more difficult it proved to reach agreement on the degree to which this power could be exercised.

Thus it proved possible to reach agreement between the (then) five Schengen partners on the power to carry out cross-border surveillance (if everything goes according to plan a discrete action for both the person being pursued and for any bystanders). But it proved impossible to reach agreement on cross-border hot pursuit which by its very nature is a more visible and aggressive action. At a Dutch initiative, the matter was brought further to the maximum feasible limit, by putting forward alternatives on the menu as it were with respect to the most sensitive aspects. In the case of cross-border hot pursuit, the Convention offers the partners the opportunity to choose whether or not to award powers of arrest to the foreign pursuers with regard to the offences to which the power applies and whether or not to set limits of time and distance as to the exercise of the power.

So much for the first angle from which we wanted to look at the internationalization of the police – the internationalization of police work. Before going any further, we should like to make a few observations regarding the structure of the consultations in the Netherlands, in preparation of international deliberations on the subject of international police cooperation. In this process, the necessity of inviting contributions from the practitioners in police work and the prosecution service is duly recognized. Such contributions guarantee, on the one hand, that as the talks evolve, their practical needs can be clearly articulated and that, right from the start, the wishes of the negiotiating partners can be discussed with those directly involved to see what effect they would have on their work. Thus, during the years of the Schengen talks, the Dutch delegation was supported by a special sub-committee of the Coordinating Police Board, comprising experts working with the CID (notably in border areas and from a number of bigger municipalities), the prosecution ser-vice and the National Criminal Information Service.

Now to the second angle from which we want to look at the internationalization of the police – the internationalization of the police organization.

III. Internationalization of Police Organization

We pointed out earlier that the police function is perceived politically and socially as one of the most manifest expressions of the sovereign state. The organization of the police within every state (in the Netherlands and surrounding countries) has taken place in different ways. In

Germany for example the police function has almost exclusively been delegated to the Länder. In France, there are two major national police organizations, the national police and the gendarmerie. The Netherlands is currently in the process of harmonizing its divided police organization into 25 regional police forces and one small national force.

III.I. The Global Perspective

The need for international police cooperation to be organized has been recognized for a long time. Even so, it is still done on the basis of co-operation between nationally-competent police organizations. Every form of institutionalization has been done on this basis, Interpol being the most obvious example. The history of the organizational structure of Interpol has already been elaborated on earlier this morning in the opening lecture. We will restrict ourselves to making a few observations about the organization from the angle of police cooperation.

It can be stated that the way Interpol is structured produces a loose and fairly non-committal grouping. With respect to this, it is interesting now to dwell briefly on the fact, that there is no convention underlying Interpol. This has consequences which, from the point of view of the Netherlands, are increasingly coming to impede Interpol's functioning and acceptance.

The absence of any underlying convention means, that the political responsibility for Interpol is unclear. Admittedly, Interpol is kept going by government contributions for which the ministers in question are accountable to their parliaments, but the highest policy-making body of Interpol, the General Assembly, is not manned by politically-accountable members of government. Thus, agreements made within Interpol retain their internal operation and do not supersede national law as do the agreements in a convention.

An example of an international institute in which the political responsibilities carry much more weight than in the case of Interpol is the consultation of Heads of Narcotic Law Enforcement Agencies under the auspices of the United Nations. Besides the Heads of the Narcotic Law Enforcement Agencies, representatives of the customs authorities and of the Ministries of Justice and Foreign Affairs also take part in the talks.

III.2. The Schengen Perspective

The question of the institutionalization of police cooperation has been considered in connection with the Convention to implement the Schengen Agreement. As we stated before, the Schengen partners adopted a very modest position on the issue of institutionalization, as they wanted to be the fore-runner of the EC Twelve and avoid any risk of conflict with the efforts being made within this broader context. This resulted in only three institutionalized bodies thin the Schengen framework i.e. the Executive Committee, Pol-Zoll and the Schengen Information System.

The first is a Committee of Ministers charged with the overall monitoring of the proper implementation of the Convention and with taking all the necessary decisions in this respect.

Pol-Zoll is a permanent consultative body of police and customs authorities which is responsible for studying joint questions relating to the combatting of drug crime and with making proposals for improving technical and practical aspects of cooperation.

And third and foremost, the Schengen Information System, a joint search system for external border checks and internal surveillance on the territories of the respective partners.

III.3. The TREVI Perspective

Since the late 1970s the Ministers of Police in the EC Member States have been holding discussions on practical police cooperation between their countries. Initially, these intergovernmental talks focused on combatting terrorism. Gradually however they have expanded to include four working groups: TREVI I which deals with matters concerning cooperation in combatting terrorism; TREVI II which looks at matters concerning training and technical equipment; TREVI III (since 1985) which is involved with matters concerning organized crime and drug crime and TREVI '92 (since 1989) which deals with matters relating to the EC-open-border-issue.

In 1989 a development relevant to the institutionalization of the police occurred in the TREVI III working party. At the TREVI III meeting of April 1989 chaired by Spain, the United Kingdom submitted a report on the desirability of national Drugs Intelligence Units in each of the Member States to improve international cooperation in combatting drug crime. These national Drugs Intelligence Units were to function as coordination referral points with different tasks and powers. Added to these proposals, was another proposal, to investigate whether at the level of the Twelve it would be possible to set up a European Drugs Intelligence Unit. The latter proposal was immediately supported by, among others, Germany.

The majority of the other delegations, the Netherlands included, which were more or less disconcerted by and unprepared for this proposal, and moreover without a mandate, were at a loss to know what to do with it. The proposal to set up national Drugs Intelligence Units was passed on to the June meeting of the TREVI Ministers in Madrid. The proposal for a study of a European Drugs Intelligence Unit failed to reach Madrid.

During the following meetings under the presidency of France (during second half of 1989) and Ireland (during the first half of 1990), reservations about a European Drugs Intelligence Unit gradually diminished. And thus in the course of TREVI '92, scope was found for including the following in the programme of action drawn up under the Irish presidency: 'Member States shall conduct a study on the need for and conditions under which it would be possible to set up a European drugs intelligence unit'. The meeting of ministers in Dublin agreed to the proposed programme of action. TREVI III was asked to report at the latest during the meeting of ministers in Luxembourg (in the first half of 1991) and if possible as early as the meeting of ministers in Rome (in the second half of 1990).

Ultimately, it was under the presidency of Luxembourg that agreement was reached on the need to arrive at a European Drugs Intelligence Unit and on the terms of reference and the specific tasks of the Unit, namely:

- Analysis of drug trafficking and drug-related crime at European level, including identification of drug trafficking organizations which by their importance could become a serious menace to the European Community;
- Collection, analysis and dissemination of data obtained from national drugs intelligence units responsible for coordination, including information on international drug trafficking investigations;
- Without prejudice to existing bilateral cooperation, to provide intelligence support to facilitate drug investigations in which at least two Member States are involved;
- Development of contacts and exchange of information with other law enforcement agencies inside and outside the EC.

Meanwhile, since the mid-1980s, the German Chancellor, Mr Kohl, has been raising eyebrows on a number of occasions in speeches which have called for a European Criminal Police Service. The concept of Europol was beginning to become manifest. His far-reaching vision is that there is actually scope for executive powers to be assigned to this body.

In June 1991 Mr Kohl, without any prior discussion in TREVI or any other forum, put a proposal to the European Council to set up Europol. We did not attend the discussion of this proposal. It is by now impossible to tell whether the members of the Council were overwhelmed by enthusiasm for it. The decision they took can only have been formulated by politicians. We quote: 'Treaty commitment to full establishment of a Central European Criminal Investigation Office (Europol) for these areas (fight against international drug trafficking and organized crime) by 31.12.1993 at the latest. Details to be laid down by unanimous decision of the Council. Gradual development of Europol functions: first of all relay station for exchange of information and experience (up to 31.12.1992), then in the second phase powers to act also within the Member States would be granted. Right of initiative for the Commission and also for individual Member States'.

Mr Kohl's comments have been studied seriously by the Dutch right from the start. In working out the details of the Schengen Convention we were already having close talks with our German neighbours. There proved to be no scope for an institution such as Europol within the Schengen Convention. At the level of the Twelve we had already experienced how difficult it had been to agree on a general study for a European Drugs Intelligence Unit as part of the programme of action. Consequently at first the Dutch government members in question took the view that there was not much scope for an institution such as Europol at the European level. For a clearer understanding of the Dutch viewpoint in this respect we shall explain the three pillars on which the evolution of the Dutch police system is based within the Dutch constitutional framework.

The first is the codifying of police powers in formal legislative frameworks. In the Netherlands above all in the criminal code and the code of criminal procedure, in the police act and in various specific acts of legislation. The second is the functioning of the police, not as an independent body, but subordinate to the competent authority (the prosecution service and the local mayor). The third pillar is the democratic check (by parliament and local municipal councils) on the authority of the police.

Looked at from this angle, it is not surprising that the Netherlands, through its government ministers, more specifically the Minister of Justice Mr Hirsch Ballin, has displayed reservations as to the creation of Europol, as envisaged by the German Chancellor, especially when it came to awarding operational powers of investigation to an institution of this kind. As Mr Hirsch Ballin stated in speeches on a number of occasions (for instance a conference in Lichtenvoorde on January 26, 1990), at present within the EC, we lack the institutional conditions for a firm system of political responsibility for the democratic and judicial control over these executive powers. Further this option would seem unattainable at present, in view of the considerable historical and cultural differences between the countries concerned. These differences are the most obvious in the different languages, but also in the differing legislation and in differing views with regard to the role of the police and the judiciary, as well as the corresponding differences in the structure and the culture of the authorities concerned. Consequently, from the Dutch point of view, the awarding of executive powers to Europol is not an issue at this stage.

The creation of a European Criminal Intelligence Service as a 'relay station for exchange of information.... ' however, seems to be feasible, also from the Netherlands point of view. This is illustrated by the Netherlands proposals on the issue during its EC presidency in de second half of 1991. The presidency proposed to the TREVI partners (who approved of it), by letter, that the study assignment with respect to the feasability of Europol, should link up with the study that was already under way on the drugs unit, and that this preliminary study should be worked out so that Europol could develop from there. The most logical way of doing this is to regard the development of the European Drugs Intelligence Unit as the first step on the road to Europol.

The TREVI Ministers undertook the study with great zeal. A fifth TREVI working party, the ad-hoc Europol group, was set up. There is an considerable time-pressure, as the first stage of Europol ('relay station for exchange of information') has to be in place by January 1, 1993. And the partners want to keep up the pressure!

First, this can be gathered from statements made during a ministers' meeting on the mafia menace in Brussels on 18 September 1992. The ministers (including the Danish minister) confirmed the seriousness of their plans regarding Europol; a request was made to the ad-hoc Europol group: 'to redouble the efforts to ensure that Europol's first phase EDU is in place by January 1993'.

In the second place this is illustrated by the fact, that beside the text we just quoted from the Treaty, a joint declaration has been agreed in which reference is made to Europol tasks with a broad scope, although not to a Europol with executive powers.

It has been agreed that, by 1994 at the latest, it will be ascertained on the basis of a report whether the breadth of cooperation within Europol has to be extended. And we are talking about an institution for which a few months after its initiation, the first stone still has to be laid.

IV. Conclusion

Europe is making rapid progress and a new phase, both politically and legally, has been embarked upon with the Treaty on European Union. It is true that objections are being voiced against the Treaty, but these objections would not seem to be directed at Art. K 1, section 9, the section regarding police cooperation.

Placed in the historical perspective described above, it has to be concluded that as of the Spanish presidency in 1989, the institutionalization of the police organization in Europe has got under way with a vengeance over a brief space of time. It was not until 1990 that there was any question of an institutionalized structure in TREVI. Now, in 1992 a treaty law basis is already being granted to Europol in the treaty on European Union.

Such an expeditious development is commendable, provided that adequate care and attention is dedicated, at national level, to a number of fundamental aspects in the process. In connection with the development of Europol care is required with regard to the following three points:

- The three pillars on which the police tasks are based in our democratic state;
- Citizens' perception of security;
- The low priority often given by the police to supra-local, let alone international tasks.

If not enough consideration is given to these domains nationally, there is the risk that the development of a broad Europol is forced upon us, that is to say a Europol with operational investigative powers, simply because practice will demand it. There is also a danger in Europol getting off to an overly rapid start, without broad support. This entails a big risk of break-up, which will put us back twenty years.

The avoidance of these risks, of this Scylla and Charybdis, will require sound piloting skills. If police organizations are also alert to what is important at European level and they do not shrink from tackling matters at that level, the channel between these mythical maelstroms will become considerably broader and thus safer. It will always be a question of navigating the straits, given citizens' just demand to know themselves to be protected.

The Dutch policy is aimed at finding the balance between the necessity of bringing about forms of police cooperation at international level (if so required, in the form of institutionalized, non-executive cooperation structures) on the one hand, and the demands for an adequate police service at national level on the other.

Police Cooperation Along the Belgian–Dutch Border

Cyrille Fijnaut

I. Introduction

The international cooperation between police forces has become the focus of interest with 'Europe 92'. The decision at the Maastricht Summit to establish a Europol shows this clearly. However, the closing of the Schengen Treaty (1985) and of the Schengen Convention (1990) by the governments of Germany, France and the Benelux Countries had already created the opening for the necessary discussion concerning this form of international cooperation. But all this should not cause one to forget that the question of international cooperation between the police forces of Belgium and the Netherlands is an old one, particularly in the border area common to both countries. All the more so as it is clearly stated in the Schengen Convention that the parties to the Convention are entitled to make further arrangements concerning cooperation in the border areas (Art. 39, Para. 4) and are further qualified either to maintain existing or to introduce new bilateral agreements of cooperation (Art. 39, Para. 5). These conditions compel one to see clearly how the execution of the existing agreements in the border areas have hitherto been organized and carried out.

Keeping in mind this connection between past and present, the arrangement of police cooperation in the Schengen Convention will shortly be discussed. Further to be discussed will be the 'police paragraph' of the Benelux Treaty of 1962 in the light of this arrangement. This discussion will be followed by an explanation regarding the settlement between the Belgian and Dutch governments in 1949 concerning the cooperation between the Dutch national police (korps rijkspolitie) and marechaussee, on the one hand, and the Belgian state police (rijkswacht), on the other. In this discussion will also be included the Schengen Convention, of course.

This account of the existing formal agreements concerning the police cooperation in the Belgian-Dutch border area will be continued with a rather lengthy account of the informal police cooperation which exists from the early 1960s under the name Nebedeag-Pol in the 'country without borders', namely, the borders of Belgium, the Netherlands and

Germany, wedged in between the towns of Aken, Luik, Verviers, Maastricht, Sittard and Heerlen. This cooperation agreement deserves a mention in this account, as it does, of course, include the Belgian-Dutch police cooperation, and further, in this area of Western Europe, at any rate, it is one of the most advanced forms of international police cooperation and, therefore, it shows an example from which lessons can be drawn in the light of the execution of the Schengen Convention, multinationally or bilaterally.

In connection with this account of Nebedeag-Pol attention is further paid to the factual cooperation which developed in the 1970s and 1980s in the Limburg-Limburg border area, and which developed unheralded during the past few years in Nebedeag-Pol and thus, in a broader sense, in the police cooperation of the Euregio Maas-Rijn. An account of the recent attempts to highlight police cooperation in the Antwerp, Noord-Brabant and Flemish border areas makes up the end of the discussion of what has been realized up to now in the Belgian-Dutch border area between the police forces concerned.

It goes without saying that in these accounts repeated references are made concerning the arrangements of police cooperation in the Schengen Convention.

II. The Formal Arrangements of Police Cooperation

II.I. The Arrangement of the Police Cooperation in the Schengen Convention

Five forms of the police cooperation can be distinguished.

To begin with, there is mention (Art. 39) of general cooperation. This one aims at mutual assistance in the course of prevention and detection of criminal offences. What this assistance will consist of has not yet been clarified. It is only stated that it should remain outside the sphere of judicial assistance and that, when it includes the exchange of written information, this information can only be given with the permission of the competent judicial authorities. Furthermore, the request to, and the giving of, assistance may in principle, only be chanelled via appointed central bodies. Who this authority is in the Netherlands and Belgium, is not mentioned in this article; according to the annexed declaration it are the Central Commissariat of the judicial police in Brussels and the Central Criminal Information Service in The Hague. Only in emergencies will the competent police authorities be allowed to assist each other directly, when so requested. The parties should otherwise, via ministerial agreements, arrange the cooperation in border areas in more detail.

Further, there is mention in the Convention of three operational forms of cooperation: the border-crossing observation (Art. 40), the border-crossing pursuit (Art. 41) and the border-crossing controlled delivery (Art. 73).

Whereas the regulation of the two first mentioned forms of cooperation is very complicated, the regulation of the last mentioned form is very simple; it includes little more than a declaration of the parties to commit themselves to this form of cooperation in the fight against the illegal trade of drugs. The conditions to be put into practice on the two other forms of cooperation are too numerous to discuss here. With reference to border-crossing observations, the most important conditions are:

- They can only take place for a relatively serious criminal offence;
- The persons in question should be reasonably suspected of complicity in the committing of such an offence;
- They should only occur with the permission (obtained before or after the event) and in accord with the instructions of a specially appointed authority;
- The officers concerned have no right to means of coercion;
- The observing officers may use their service weapon only in case of dire necessity.

The conditions governing border-crossing pursuits are similar:

- They can only be carried out against a person found to be committing or assisting in certain named criminal offences, or offences which may lead to extradition;
- They cannot be taken over in time by the authorities of the other party;
- They can only be carried out by police officers in uniform; those may carry their service weapon, but may use it only in dire emergencies;
- They should occur only in close cooperation with the competent foreign authorities;
- They may take place only at the time and place as agreed between the parties concerned.

In the third place, there is mention of an important informative form of cooperation (Art. 46). This article shows that a party, in individual cases, without being so requested, may send another party information which may be of interest to it in helping prevent future crime or to avert offences against or threats to public order and security. The exchange of information in this connection should in principle be handled through a central body, except in urgent situations.

Fourthly: the parties are obliged (Art. 44) to instal the necessary means of communication, especially in the border areas, with a view to prompt cooperation between police and customs.

In the fifth place, there is a personnel form of cooperation (Art. 47). This means that liaison officers can be detached to police services of the other party. They have only an advisory and assistance task.

The Arts. 126 up to and including Art. 130 further give several directives concerning the protection of personal data, which, via the above-mentioned forms of cooperation, could be exchanged. Most important here, is that Art. 129 demands of the parties that they provide a level of protection that satisfies the principles of Recommendation R (87) 15 of the Committee of Ministers of the Council of Europe dated 17-09-1987 concerning the use of personal data by police forces.

Finally, it should be noted that Arts. 42 and 43 provide a legal position to the officers who, in the framework of a pursuit or observation action, cross the border: they are, with respect to possible offences committed against or by them, on a par with the officers of the party on whose territory they operate. This ruling also covers provision for compenzation, for damage, which they might cause during their stay on that territory.

II. 2. The Arrangement of Police Cooperation in the Benelux Treaty

Speaking of the influence of the Benelux Treaty concerning extradition and mutual assistance in criminal cases of 1962 and modified by Protocol of 1974, on the arrangement of cooperation in the Schengen Convention, one could – in the light of the goals of this Convention – possibly be inclined to call into question the worth of the Convention concerning the administrative and judicial cooperation in the area of the arrangements related to the realization of the goals of the Benelux Economical Union of 1969. In this Convention are, within the framework of the mutual assistance concerning criminal offences, many forms of police cooperation which go much further than mentioned in the Treaty. And these forms of cooperation in addition correspond much more closely with the ultimate goals of Schengen. Yet, there is not a bit of influence of this Convention on the realization of the Schengen Convention. Perhaps not, on the one hand, because the Schengen partners were completely 'sold' on cooperation between the regular police services and, on the other hand, because the here-mentioned Benelux Convention has lost much of its practical meaning as a result of the evolution of the European Community.[1]

The regulation of police cooperation in the first-mentioned Benelux Treaty concerns mainly the border-crossing pursuit. This pinpoints immediately the most important difference between this arrangement and the one shown in the Schengen Convention: there is no mention anywhere of the other forms of operational cooperation. This is not really remarkable – in view of the existence of the police cooperation agreements, to be discussed later. In other words, one could consider the Benelux Treaty and these agreements as being complementary to each other.

To be able to compare the arrangement of the border-crossing pursuit in the Benelux Treaty with the one in the Schengen Convention, it should be understood that according to Art. 26, Para. 1, appointed police officers of one party can be deputized by their own judicial authorities to operate on the territory of another party with the permission of the competent officer of that party's prosecution service, in order to assist with the investigation and detection of crimes. To this end, these officers will be issued with a rogatory commission stating its purpose. In Para. 2 is added that the named officers will give all the necessary information which could be useful to execute satisfactorily the task required.

Art. 27, Para. 1, continues: the officers of one party who in their own country pursue a person suspected of having committed an offence which might result of extradition are authorized, while in pursuit, to enter the territory of another party. They are immediately required to inform the competent authorities of that party; these in turn should, when

1. Important comments on this Treaty are: Constant, J., 'Le traité Benelux d'extradition et d'entraide judiciaire en matière pénal du 27 juin 1962', *Journal des Tribunaux*, 1962, no. 4372, 489-497; De Schutter, B., 'L'entraide judiciaire en matière pénale dans le cadre du Benelux', *Belgisch Tijdschrift voor Internationaal Recht*, 1967, no. 1, 102-126, and 'Samenwerking in strafzaken en pogingen tot harmonisatie van het strafrecht in de Beneluxlanden', in: *Droit pénal européen, Europees strafrecht, European criminal law*, Bruxelles, 1970, 569-597 and 'International criminal cooperation; the Benelux example', in: Bassiouni, M.Ch., ed., *A Treatise on International Criminal Law*, Springfield, Ill.: Charles C. Thomas, 1973, V.2, 249-260; Schutte J.J.E. and Thomas F., *Preadviezen over uitlevering en de wederzijdse rechtshulp in strafzaken*, Zwolle: W.E.J. Tjeenk Willink, 1977. Concerning the role of this Treaty in the evolution of police cooperation in Western Europe see Fijnaut, C., 'Police Cooperation within Western Europe', in: Freidensohn, F. and Farrell, M., eds., *Crime in Europe*, London: Routledge, 1991, 116-117 and Geysels, F., 'Benelux: the Forerunner of the European Community in the Field of the Free Movement of Persons across International Frontiers?', *The Police Journal*, 1990, no. 2, 103-120.

so requested, stop the pursued in order to establish his identity, or to arrest him. This general rule is, however, limited to special cases as shown in Para. 2 of this article: if the pursuit is not interrupted and the need for speed during the pursuit makes it impossible to contact the local authorities, then the officers of the other party, within a ten kilometers zone of the border, may themselves stop the pursued person and bring him before the local authorities. Added to this Para. 3 states: where necessary, the case will then proceed as stated in Art. 26, even if the rogatory commission is not present.[2] Finally, in Para. 4, is stated who the competent officers are: members of the judicial police, the Belgian and Dutch state police and the members of the municipal police belonging to municipalities whose territories are less than ten kilometers from the border.

There are finally, in Art. 28, a number of conditions concerning the various forms of border crossings with reference to the Arts. 26 and 27. First, that the officers in question are on a par with the officers of the other party, when acting on the territory of that party, concerning criminal offences of which they were the victims, or which they had perpetrated. Secondly, they should at any time be able to show their credentials. Thirdly, that they may be in uniform, when they operate in the framework of Art. 27, including the possession of any weapons belonging to their function. And finally, in case of dire emergency, that they may use force under the same conditions as permitted to the officers of the party on whose territory the action is taking place.

Should one now wish to make a comparison with the Schengen Convention at this point, then it is clear that the arrangement concerning the right to pursuit between the Benelux Treaty and the Schengen Convention shows a number of important differences. And not just differences, but differences which show that the last-mentioned Convention is much more restrictive than the first-mentioned. Reference the fact that, according to the Schengen Convention, pursuit is only permitted when the other party cannot in time take over the pursuit, that pursuit is only permitted in the case of 'caught in the act', that only in the case of 'dire emergency' the officer may use his weapon and is not permitted to use other forceful means, and that higher authority is needed to sanction the whole course of pursuit, from the beginning to the end. There are, of course, also similarities, for instance, the legal position of officers who, while on foreign territory, commit offences or fall victim to the offences of others.

2. Bruggeman, W., 'Cross border observation', in: Fijnaut, C. and Hermans, R., eds., *Police Cooperation in Europe*, Lochem: J.B. van den Brink, 1987, 59-64.

This comparison is not without interest for the interpretation of Arts. 26 and 27 of the Benelux Treaty. Where the text of the corresponding articles in the Schengen Convention (Arts. 40 and 41) simply excludes that the ruling, concerning the border-crossing pursuit, also contains an arrangement concerning border-crossing observation – one finds the text of the relevant articles in the Benelux Treaty rather mysterious on this point. This is not as strange as it may seem: when this agreement was drawn up, there was, as there is now, no question of systematical observation. But, now that such observation does exist, and while the Treaty has not been changed in the meanwhile, one asks, if, and if so, under what conditions, the border-crossing observation in the frame of the Benelux Treaty is possible. The answer to this question is not clear in any one of the countries concerned. Not disputed is, I believe, that according to Art. 26 and, possibly, Art. 27, cross-border observation is possible. The provision in Art. 26 that officers of another party are authorized to assist with the detection of offences is generally considered to be an acceptable basis for such action.

The problem is, however, how freely should such action be taken! More precise: also forms of observation which should not result in tracking down criminals and/or the detection of criminal offences: Strategic observation in other words? And if this is not so – and this form of observation has therefore not to satisfy the conditions as laid down in Art. 26, namely the prior issuing of a rogatory commission by a judicial authority – which condition should then be satisfied?

The Dutch State Secretary of Justice, in December 1984, has as a result of a conflict with the Belgian government about the actions of a Dutch observation group on Belgian territory, informed the attorneys-general and the public prosecutors, that there exists no doubt in de Benelux Treaty that action on foreign territory, including observation, is only possible with prior permission from the competent authorities of the party concerned and that, therefore, agreements at police level are not sufficient.

Finally, it is of interest to note that the execution of the right to pursue is, according to the Benelux Treaty, not really limited to place or time. Concerning the competent officers, there has only been drawn a ten kilometer boundary with respect to members of the municipal police, not with respect to the judicial police or the state police forces. And concerning the execution of this right, the Treaty only states that, subject to certain conditions, a.o. the ten kilometer zone, the officers in question have authority to stop a subject after uninterrupted pursuit. The Treaty does not at all exclude police officers, particularly state police officers, to pursue suspects outside the ten kilometer zone, of course, subject to certain conditions, such as notification to the competent authorities of another party.

Compared with the arrangement in the Schengen Convention, it should be noted that there is in this arrangement no mention of a territorial boundary limiting competent police officers authorized to cross-boundary pursuit. It also shows clearly in Para. 3 of Art. 41 of the Schengen Convention that the parties concerned were not at all in agreement about the – let us say – functional limitations of the execution of the right to pursuit across the border. This paragraph binds the parties to state either one of two forms of declaration: there is to be a certain zone or time limit from the place or the time where the border is crossed, or there is to be no limitation at all in respect of time or distance. The Dutch and Belgian governments have hereto declared that their police officers will be bound by the rules as laid down in Art. 27 of the Benelux Treaty, in as far as it concerns pursuits on Belgian-Dutch territories.

II.3. The Arrangement of Police Cooperation in the Belgian-Dutch Border Area

Informal, even secret cooperation between police forces has always existed in Europe, certainly at political level but also on a criminal plane.[3] The first formal agreements, be they only at governmental level, date back only as far as the last ten years of the previous century and the first ten years of this century. More specific, we are here concerned about agreements regarding the cooperation in the border area between the police forces of the various countries. Thus, in 1891, an agreement was concluded concerning cooperation between the Belgian state police and the Prussian gendarmerie, in 1910 an agreement about cooperation between the Belgian state police and the Dutch state police, in 1919 one concerning the cooperation between the French gendarmerie and the Belgian gendarmerie, and in 1920 one between the Luxembourg gendar-

3. See in general Fijnaut, C., *Opdat de macht een toevlucht zij; Een historische studie van het politieapparaat als een politieke instelling*, Antwerpen-Arnhem: Kluwer Rechtswetenschappen – Gouda Quint, 1979, 2 vol. Some of the more important publications on police cooperation are: Siemann, W., *Deutschlands Ruhe, Sicherheit und Ordnung*, Tubingen: Max Niemeyer, 1985; Porter, B., *The Origins of the Vigilant State*, London: Weidenfeld and Nicolson, 1987; Johnson, R.J., *The Okhrana Abroad, 1885-1917*, Colombia University, 1970.

merie and the Belgian state police. All this came about from earlier existing practices.[4]

When one compares the content of these agreements with those of the Schengen Convention, it seems to be that time has either stood still, or has passed on only very slowly. The police forces concerned obtained the authority to exchange information and to carry out observations on known offenders hanging about the frontiers. Their members were permitted to cross the frontiers armed and in uniform when it was felt necessary, and, in the case of self-defence, weapons could be used. They were not authorized to stop and search suspects on foreign soil, but they were authorized to ask their foreign colleagues to set in motion the necessary action when suspected serious offenders still were on their territory. The only real important difference, concerning the actual border crossing action, is, therefore, only the power to stop a person – which according to the Schengen Convention can be arranged bilaterally between the parties. In short, he who thinks there is something new in the Schengen Convention, where it covers the police exchange of information and mutual police assistance, does not know what he is talking about.

These agreements have, of course, become dated with the passing of time. One only needs to think of the radical transformations which were undergone by the police systems of the countries engaged in, and after the Second World War and of the growth of international legal assistance in Europe, outside the framework of extradition. They have not, or not totally, lost their practical meaning since that time, however. Some of these agreements, such as those concerning the cooperation in the Belgian-French and the Belgian-Luxembourg border areas, still form the basis for all kinds of practical cooperation between the police forces on both sides of the border. Equally so, the agreement concerning cooperation between the Dutch state police and marechaussee and the Belgian gendarmerie and judicial police which was reviewed in 1949, after the example of the Franco-Belgian agreement.

Let us now compare the relevant articles of the Benelux Treaty with this Agreement from 1949. It instructs the commanding officers of the forces in question to consult with each other regularly and, furthermore, depending on the degree of urgency, to organize meetings between the brigades opposite each other on the border. In addition the units con-

4. See the report of Dierkens, R., Bruggeman, W., De Ruyter, B. and Zanders, P., *Grensoverschrijdende criminaliteit*, Gent: Rijksuniversiteit te Gent, School voor Criminologie, 1991, 405-411, and Van den Hoek, W., *De geschiedenis van het Wapen der Koninklijke Marechaussee*, 's-Gravenhage: Stichting Ons Wapen, 1963, 277-278.

cerned are obliged to send each other data concerning suspects who either live in, or hang about the border. They are also to warn each other in the event of crimes or other serious offences in the border areas. According to the Agreement having received such a warning, an active investigation should be set up by the police force concerned, in order to track down the criminals and the proceeds of their crime, if any. This Agreement also authorises the members of the forces in question to cross the border in uniform in execution of their duty after having identified themselves. An 'addendum' explains that 'in execution of their duty' does not permit them to the right of pursuit. Neither are they permitted to carry weapons on foreign territory.

This Agreement, which formed the starting point for fruitful cooperation between the police forces in the Limburg-Limburg border area, in particular in connection with the formerly mentioned articles of the Benelux Treaty, offers, of course, interesting material for comparison with the Schengen Convention. First of all, it could be pointed out that the Agreement is really only meant to regulate the police cooperation in the common border area and not, as in the Schengen Convention, the cooperation, in general, between the police forces in the countries concerned.

It should also be noted that the Agreement only concerns the cooperation between the state police faces in the common border area and does not cover the possible cooperation in this connection between local police forces, or between these forces and the state police forces, not forgetting the judicial police. Further, it should be clear that the Agreement does permit border crossing by police officers but does not permit border crossing executive police action, and even in the event of cross-border meetings they are not authorized to carry weapons. Finally, this Agreement does not mention technical and personnel cooperation, nor does it mention the legal position of police officers who cross the border.

In considering which similarities are relevant here, there is one clearly showing the liberal arrangement for the exchange of information concerning suspects and the resulting obligation, in some cases, to render assistance to track them down; the Agreement does not cover, of course, the protection of personal data which might be exchanged. And although this point of conformity suggests that this Agreement is as judicially orientated as the relevant passages in the Schengen Convention, it should be understood that the Agreement explicitly also is aimed to ensure good policing in the border areas in general. The other similarity is, that this Agreement does not place these various forms of cooperation under the control of higher authority, at least, not directly.

They are completely in the hands of the police forces concerned. Final authority rests, of course, with the various governments, in accordance with their laws.

III. Factual Forms of Police Cooperation

III.1. Some General Remarks

Before discussing the factual forms of police cooperation, one by one, as mentioned in the introduction, some general remarks should be made about the application of the Benelux Treaty and the Agreement of 1949. The extent of these conventions is certainly not limited to the localities where they have been applied to their utmost.

The first remark to be made is, that, up to today, no systematic study has been made of the application of these conventions. This, as I have argued years ago, is a sad state of affairs in the light of possible future developments. From various sources, it becomes clear, that in practice the Benelux Treaty is not strictly enforced or, at least, the narrow explanation that has been given by higher authority in some cases; stories are circulating, for instance, about foreign police officers who have stopped and searched suspects after pursuit reaching far beyond the ten kilometer limit, this on their own initiative and carrying weapons. One is not always in possession of a rogatory commission, either before or after, when engaged in cross-border observation. It is, however, the usual custom, when crossing the border, to inform the Central Bureau for Investigation (CBO) of the Belgian state police or the Central Criminal Information Service (CRI) and also the prosecution service concerned in connection with the continuation of the observation (either combined or by one party only). Dutch observation groups usually cover themselves against possible civic actions in this connection, by obtaining from their prosecution service an official travel order conforming to the rules as laid down in 1983 with respect to international judicial assistance. Other activities also occur in the border area about which no mention is made in the Benelux Treaty, such as the interviewing of a suspect on a police officer's own initiative.

In the second place, it can be established, by means of archival material, that the 1949 Agreement has led to the development of a precise system of consultation between the brigades and districts of the Belgian state police and the Dutch state police all along the Belgian/Dutch border. However, this system has obviously become weaker since the 1950s.

Thirdly, it is therefore important to note that only in recent times organized consultation between police forces is again taking place, along the whole common border, in one form or another. This consultation in the area of the provinces Luik and (Belgian-Dutch) Limburg takes place along the channel of Nebedeag-Pol. As far as the area of the provinces North-Brabant and Antwerp is concerned, there has recently been created a common work-group which is studying the possibilities and difficulties of police cooperation in this border area. And a few years ago, in the Flemish border area, there also has been created a monthly discussion group, be it only limited to the exchange of information concerning the fight against serious crime.

In the fourth place, the only form of systematic cooperation now existing in the total mutual border area, is the one which was set up in 1973 (and amended regularly ever since) for the arranging and operating of 'police-alarm'. A request to activate this alarm can only be made in the case of a very serious, non-political, criminal offence, where there are grounds to believe that the suspect(s) has (have) bolted to Belgium (or Holland) and when there are sufficient reasons for observation or arrest. Furthermore, each request should also contain a request for the temporary detaining of the suspect(s) in the sense of the Benelux Treaty. The details of this (confidential) arrangement are outside the scope of this report.

Finally, it follows that when one wants to know what the police cooperation between Belgium and Holland really means, one cannot limit this search to a specific area of the border. Not only because the scale of cooperation differs greatly from area to area but also because this cooperation, however and wherever practized, is influenced to a certain extent by common regulations.

III.2. The Organization and Working of Nebedeag-Pol

That a lot of attention is paid to the organization and working of the police cooperation in the Dutch – German – Belgian border area, usually referred to as inner area, the centre, of the Euregio Maas-Rijn, has many reasons.

The first one is, that Nebedeag-Pol could be characterized as the most successful example of the (territorially based) cooperation agreements which, during the 1960s and 1970s, were created in this part of Europe, compared to e.g. the Cross Channel Conference attended by police officers from England, France, Belgium and Holland. The second reason is that Nebedeag-Pol should be seen as one of the most important sources of experience from which possible future bilateral agreements on the basis of the Schengen Convention can be drawn up. And, thirdly, that Nebedeag-Pol will form the starting point from which, possibly at Euro-Regional level, police cooperation can be set up.

The pre-history of Nebedeag-Pol goes back to the 1920s. More form and content came about, however, after World War II, in the 'Land without borders'. Police officers from Vaals (state police), Verviers (judicial police) and Aken sought contact with each other in order to fight the professional, sometimes violent, smuggling bands. There is no doubt that these contacts were intensified and structured under the influence of the German-Belgian and German-Dutch agreements dated June-July '60 concerning police cooperation, but also under the influence of the arrangements for police cooperation in the Benelux Treaty of 1962.[5]

With the result that the then police president of Aken, E. Dundalek, thought it time to organize the more or less loose connections on a more official basis. He, therefore, invited the police chiefs from the border area between Aken, Luik, Verviers, Maastricht, Sittard and Heerlen to a meeting on 17-09-69 and, together with them, established the 'Arbeitsgemeinschaft der Leiter der Polizeidiensstellen im Belgisch-Niederländisch-Deutschen Grenzgebiet'. The immediate goals of this working party were: to increase, mutually, the knowledge of the police organization, to organize language courses for police officers, to instal direct radio and telex-communications, to appoint liaison officers and to arrange for the exchange of information concerning crime and criminals.[6]

Some points of this programme were, more or less, realized in the years following their adoption. The desired forms of communication were established first. A work group designed a form in three languages for the mutual reporting of crimes and criminals. The exchange of detection reports and dayly reports was regulated. Intensive consultation between forces concerning the fight against drug trafficking was set up. It also became possible to become involved in the detection of serious crimes committed on foreign soil, this via 'duty tours' as mentioned in Art. 14 of the German-Dutch Agreement of 03-06-60.[7]

The wish for further cooperation, especially from the German side, grew stronger at the same time. The then police president of Aken,

5. See Ghelen, 'Polizeiliche Zusammenarbeit im Aachener Grenzraum', in: *10 Jahre Arbeitsgemeinschaft der Niederländischen, Belgischen und Deutschen Polizeiverwalter im Aachener Grenzgebiet*, Aachen: Polizeipräsidium, 1979, 10-15.
6. Junge, H., and Weiss, K., 'Koordinierte Verbrechensbekämpfung', *Kriminalistik*, 1972, no. 11, 530-533.
7. Salewsky, F., 'Die Deutsch-Niederländische Arbeitsgruppe zur Bekämpfung der Rauschgiftkriminalität", *Kriminalistik*, 1977, no. 9, 403-406.

F. Fehrmann, published his list of requirements in 1975 in *Die Polizei*. He wanted pursuit across the German-Dutch and German-Belgian borders made possible, in accord with Art. 27 of the Benelux Treaty. He also thought that police officers should be authorized, with the permission and presence of local authorities, to interview suspects, to search premises and to confiscate goods, on foreign territory.[8] Furthermore, it appeared to him that evidence obtained at the request of foreign police forces should, in certain circumstances, immediately be returned to the country of origin. However, as he told me, most of this did not come about in the following years. Despite all efforts it proved to be impossible to reconstruct the German-Belgian and the German-Dutch agreement after the model of the German-French agreement concerning mutual police cooperation of 1977. Let alone that it appeared to be possible to lift the arrangement concerning police cooperation to a higher plan in the Dutch-German border area within the framework of the German-Dutch agreement of 30-8-79 concerning the completion and simplification of the execution of the European Treaty *re* the mutual legal assistance in criminal cases of 20-4-59. The only concrete result that F. Fehrmann (in 1979) achieved was that the working party obtained the statute of a private association following German law. Why he, and his supporters, failed in their further endeavours, is not clear. It is known, however, in certain circles, that a number of Dutch police officers, mindful of the past, did not want to be as 'go-ahead' as F. Fehrmann and Co. With hindsight, however, it is more important to note that their wishes have been absorbed as it were, by the political discussions, during the 1980s, which eventually led to the Schengen Convention.

One might think that this development has somewhat overshadowed the evolution of Nebedeag-Pol. Yet it has not become less important when one considers the execution of the Schengen Treaty and Schengen Convention. Lessons can be learned from its factual evolution, as has been said, for the future effecting of bilateral agreements within the framework of Schengen Convention.

If one considers what has been realized in the last few years, supplementary to what already had been established in the 1970s, one should mention in the first place the organization of an annual study week for members of the middle ranks of the police forces concerned. Furthermore, for some time now, efforts have been, and are being, made to establish a single police alarm system for the whole of the German –

8. Fehrmann, F., 'Probleme der grenznachbarlichen polizeilichen Zusammenarbeit', *Die Polizei*, 1975, no. 4, 118-122.

Dutch – Belgian border area. And finally, serious attempts are being made to develop a common crime prevention policy.

Speaking operationally, however, the most notable result during the past few years has been the cooperation in the sphere of cross-border observation. As the existing conventions are silent on this subject, agreements have been made among the parties concerned about the conditions and ways in which observation can be carried out (for instance: the carrying of weapons and the reporting of border crossings) or be handed over. Structural discussions between leaders of observation teams and annual exercises have not only exposed many technical and tactical problems, but also contributed to solving them. There are also signs that there is a real desire for the creation of international observation teams, be it only on an ad-hoc basis for the time being.

It should finally be said that, because the parties have got to know each other really well in the past few years, there are usually no problems when police officers find themselves on foreign soil while engaged in pursuit actions.

When the above mentioned discussions and developments are compared with the arrangements of police cooperation in the Schengen Convention, one cannot fail to notice a very much mixed result. In the first place, it can be seen that a number of operational, technical and personnel results of Nebedeag-Pol can be easily integrated in the modalities of cooperation which are provided in the Convention. This integration will, however, cause problems on 3 points: 1) The exchange of personal data, 2) the cross-border observation to obtain information and, 3) the inclusion of central authorities such as the Bundeskriminalamt and the Commissariat General of the judicial police; up to date, these authorities played no part in Nebedeag-Pol, at least no meaningful role. Secondly, the Schengen Convention, at least partly, meets the wishes of F. Fehrmann and other German police functionaries in respect of the possibilities of further actions *re* border-crossing. This part concerns the arrangements concerning the right to pursuit. The other part concerns the interviewing of suspects and witnesses, the searching of premises, etc. without the need of a judicial request for a warrant; this remained outside the police cooperation arrangements. Lastly, it should be noted that certain developments in Nebedeag-Pol are outside the Schengen Convention as such, for instance, the organization of a common alarm system.

Having reached this point, it would be wise to touch upon the entanglements between Nebedeag-Pol and Euregio Maas-Rijn. There has been a bond between this Euregio, from its creation in the early 1980s, and Nebedeag-Pol. The aforementioned F. Fehrmann, chairman of

Nebedeag-Pol for years, was also the first chairman of the Arbeitsgruppe Offentliche Sicherheit und Ordnung. This work group has been particularly concerned with the cross-border activities of fire brigades, ambulance services, etc. during the past few years. The reason for this is not difficult to see: police cooperation was looked after by Nebedeag-Pol, at least in the centre of this Euregio. This did not mean that the growth of the Euregio did not touch this police cooperation arrangement.

Its development, in fact, led to the increase of the number of participants in its activities; first, in the 1960s, they came mainly from the area Aken, Sittard, Maastricht and Verviers, but since 1988 they came also from Belgian Limburg as well and from the German area above Aken. Secondly, a number of activities of Nebedeag-Pol is at present financed by the Euregio, such as the annual study week. And, in the near future, in view of the decisions which were taken on 24-11-90 at a Euro-Regional meeting of town councils of the most important towns: Aken, Hasselt, Heerlen, Maastricht and Luik, it is not likely to be limited this way. It was, in fact, decided at that meeting, that a strong cooperation was necessary in the field of public order, safety and the fight against crime.

It almost goes without saying that such a development could cause tension between Euregio and Nebedeag-Pol on the one hand, and, on the other hand, with the execution of the judicially orientated Schengen Convention. An easy solution of these potential conflicts is not on the horizon. They are too much interwoven with the contrasts between the administrative, judicial and police frameworks within which they have developed.

III.3. The Factual Cooperation in the Limburg-Limburg Border Area in the 1970s and 1980s

In this area, too, it was, in 1949-1950, stipulated, as to place time and person, how the cross-border cooperation between the state police forces (Dutch and Belgian) and the marechaussee should be executed, in accordance with the 1949 Agreement. However, this system too, as is shown in earlier correspondence, has deteriorated with time. Only at district level, around 1970, were there regular 3 monthly consultations, in relation to criminal information.

This cooperation, on the initiative of W. Schaafsma, commanding officer of the Dutch state police in the Maastricht area, was given a new lease of life in 1975. The district commanders of the state police in Limburg and North Brabant-East, the district commanders of the state police in Belgian Limburg, the chiefs of the local police forces in Dutch Limburg and the divisional commander of the marechaussee (at Breda) came together in Hasselt for the first time, in June of that year, to discuss how to improve on the mutual cooperation in accordance with the Benelux Treaty and the Agreement of 1949. The chief of police of Hasselt was also invited, at a later stage. But, neither the other local police chiefs in Belgian Limburg nor the heads of the judicial police in that area have ever participated. The Belgians, for whatever reason, held strictly to the Agreement of 1949 in this connection. Judicial and administrative authorities have never directly been involved, as mentioned earlier; they were, however, occasionally consulted in the background.

These discussions were held once or twice a year mostly on Dutch, but sometimes on Belgian territory. Over the years a number of subjects were shown on the agenda: the execution of the police alarm, the application of the law of pursuit, the organization of common border controls, the organizing of periodical, regional CID meetings, the signifying of alternative routes at traffic detours, the creation of a common warning system for cross-border activities, the exchange of information about the maintaining of order at large-scale demonstrations, the organization and work method of arrest teams, etc., etc. And it did not stop at talking. A hand plasticized instruction has been developed for practical daily use with a resume of the 'Belgian – Dutch arrangement concerning the right of pursuit beyond the border'. The regional CID meetings have arrived; one up to today (in the area Eindhoven, Valkenswaard, Lommel and Leopoldsburg). Also, the direct radio contacts across the border have been improved considerably.

Set against the arrangement of police cooperation in the Benelux Treaty, it is self evident that the previously mentioned discussion has developed well beyond this Treaty. Not only because it covered important aspects of the administrative police function, but also because it was supported, from a judicial viewpoint, by the aforementioned bilateral Agreement between Belgium and Holland, which makes some forms of cooperation possible, such as regular consultation concerning criminal investigation, that is not mentioned in the Benelux Treaty. Roughly the same conclusion can be reached when one compares these discussions and their result with the arrangement of police cooperation in the Schengen Convention – as far as this comparison goes; bilateral agreements can still be created according to this Convention.

Also then becomes apparent how limited this Convention is from an administrative point of view and how limited also from a judicial viewpoint, particularly when one includes in this comparison the practice that has developed in the meantime about the cross-border observation.

For instance, no noticeable room has been created in this Convention for the systematic exchange of CID information, nor does it offer explicit possibilities, as mentioned before, for strategic forms of cross-border observation. Further still, it introduces a totally new ruling for the protection of personal data. In short, all this confirms again, that the Schengen Convention not only legalizes existing police practices, it also regulates them.

Half way through the 1980s this cooperation pact ceased to exist as such, that, seen from a territorial point of view, was a freely complementary adjunct of Nebedeag-Pol. This should mainly be attributed to the fact that its pacemakers by then had left the police service. The further development of the Euregio Maas-Rijn and thereby the broadening of the police cooperation across the borders of the 'land without frontiers', has certainly also played a part in this. For these developments brought all police forces in the South of (Belgian) Limburg within the sphere of influence of Nebedeag-Pol. The arranged cooperation between the police services in the North of this province, around Leopoldsburg in particular, and in the East of North Brabant, particularly, the local police and the state police of Eindhoven, came to a standstill. The only few contacts still remaining are between the CID units.

III.4. The Recent Growth of Police Cooperation in the Provinces Antwerp, Belgian Limburg and North Brabant

The once organized border discussion in this area has also virtually disappeared. The incidental contacts are few and/or of a personal nature. It was decided some years ago, in the framework of the Belgian-Dutch Border Conference (Benego), an exclusive administratively orientated cooperation pact, to charge a special work group with the development of police discussion structures, but such a work group has not yet been instituted.

However, a working group has been established in 1991, on the initiative of the chiefs of the municipal police of Eindhoven and Tilburg, following a meeting of the collective police chiefs in the province of North Brabant, that has to improve police cooperation between the forces in the provinces of North Brabant and Antwerp and the area around Hasselt. This working group consists of a representative of the Dutch state police, Breda district, and a representative of, respectively, the municipal police of Eindhoven and Tilburg. There will also be a representative from the state police, Brasschaat district, a representative from the judicial police of, respectively, the brigades of Antwerp, Turnhout and Hasselt and, lastly, a representative of the municipal forces of Antwerp, Turnhout and Hasselt; all from Belgium. Consequently, all police forces have been united within this working group.

The task mandate concerns itself with the total (operational) police cooperation in this area and does not limit itself to judicial frameworks. The daily individual contacts between police officers across the border serve as a basic model, the goal set to the work group is to formulate proposals for a good and clear interpretation of the existing mutual aid treaties, as mentioned above. The prosecution services concerned of both countries need to give their permission hereto.

The working group needs to break through the ad-hoc character which permeates the present cooperation in order to form a solid base which will facilitate the implementation of the Schengen Convention. It is also important that the work group should contribute to the growing trust between the police forces and should noticeably improve the knowledge of each others organizations and judicial systems.

Although there is also police cooperation concerning public order and the fight against disasters, the judicial cooperation is the most important subject at the moment because of the fact that here is the greatest possible gain. Here is shown most clearly the ad-hoc character and it also shows that the cooperation is too much determined by the individual acts of police officers and representatives of the judiciary, in spite of the possibility of the mutual aid treaties.

Unhappily, there is not yet a real cooperation culture in this area. Concrete examples shows this clearly. In some criminal investigations where both Holland and Belgium had an interest, no positive result came about. In recent murder investigations, it was not possible to set up a common investigation team for instance, despite the fact that it was possible, from a legal viewpoint. There was no lack of mutual assistance but, because of continual circulation of officers who, always on an adhoc basis, were to carry out this assistance, these investigations have been closed without arrests. A standing team of Belgian and Dutch CID officers, comparable with the Dutch assistance teams, is no guarantee for a good result, but presently great gaps appear in investigations through lack of operational cohesion.

The investigations in question illustrate how fragile and inept the present cooperation is, they show the difference of the working methods between the police forces and how little they know of each other. They also show how large the degree of success enjoyed by international criminals is, and that the abolishment of border controls is not the most important factor in this respect. The border appears to be a barrier for the police and judiciary only, even after this magical year of '1992'. Herein lies the most important task for the working group. Not only in the making of arrangements *re* the lower and upper margin of police cooperation but also in the fostering of a cooperation culture on the basis of mutual respect and trust, including the officers of the judiciary. The working group should use the structure of Nebedeag-Pol in Limburg as a guide.

The concrete subjects of the police cooperation do not differ from those of other inter-regional cooperation arrangements. The communications, common controls, pursuits, border almanac and exchange of data are also on the agenda here. The last named subject, especially, is most important. It appears from the data of the police services on both sides of the border that the same problems exist in the border areas: car crimes, burglaries, raids, etc. There are indications that the same groups are committing these crimes. Notably Dutch criminals commit all kinds of crimes pertaining to property across the border. Up to now, it has remained impossible to exchange information hereof across the border. It is the working group task, as one of its first acts and on the basis of the Dutch legislation concerning police registers, to provide the Belgian police services with relevant criminal information, this of course with ministerial permission.

A more difficult subject will be the clear interpretation of the mutual aid treaties, particularly the Benelux Treaty. As mentioned before, in the Art. 26, etc. are sufficient possibilities to result, in the framework of the execution of commissions rogatory, in fruitful cooperation. Agreements concerning these possibilities should be supported by the relevant prosecution services in order that the fight against crime in the border area will no longer depend on the personal views of an individual police chief or magistrate. Herein lies one of the problems with which the working group struggles at the moment. Although the police cooperation has much political attention, thanks to the development of Schengen, there still remains the question whether affairs which are outside of the control of police authorities will be solved by higher authorities. Administrative affairs could possibly be dealt with within the BENEGO connection for instance, but as to judicial affairs the process to follow is not that clear. This is because the Belgian police structure concerning the judicial police function and particularly the relations between the state police and the judicial police, could lead to obscure situations. Neither is there structural consultation, in whatever form, between representatives of the prosecution services in Holland and Belgium; there are only incidental contacts between the attorneys general of Antwerp and 's-Hertogenbosch. It is also felt as a handicap that the Belgian representatives have barely mandate to make arrangements.

Nevertheless, a movement has now been started involving all police activities, territorially as well as professionally. The activities of, and the atmosphere in, the working group give hope to the expectation that its task will be fulfilled provided that the exchange of information and experience in the form of stages will generate sufficient trust. Of even greater interest will be the consequences of the working group activities, in police circles but also in government circles and the judiciary.

III.5. The First Contacts Regarding the Structuring of Police Cooperation in Zeeland, East Flanders and West Flanders

Also in the area containing the provinces Zeeland, East Flanders and West Flanders the first contacts have recently been made to structure the cooperation between police services, especially with a view to Schengen. The daily cooperation between the police services in this border area is strong and correct but here also is the impression, fostered by experience, that more should be possible, as earlier mentioned. A working group has therefore been set up, consisting of representatives of the Dutch state police and a representative of the Belgian state police, to ponder the same problems as those mentioned in the previous paragraph. Communication has been sought by this working group with the working group of North Brabant and Antwerp. Exchanges of information are to be made between these groups, but they are to operate independently in order to save the local colour of each others territory and to control the organizational developments.

IV. Conclusion

The police cooperation in the Belgian-Dutch border area is – as has been shown – a rather complicated question and presents a rather motley entity. It is therefore not surprising that the many comparisons between (existing) formal arrangements and factual forms on the one side, and the arrangements in the Schengen Convention on the other side, demonstrate a number of many sized differences. Where in one area it falls short of what has been formally agreed, or in fact exists, in another area, it offers a widespread range of unknown possibilities. The least that can be said for this Convention is, that, after ratification (let us not forget this!) it will exercise a strong structural and regulating influence on the police cooperation in all the border areas.

To what degree it will do this depends of course, before anything else, on the political and official will in the countries concerned. There will need to be much expenditure of energy to solve satisfactorily the numerous judicial, financial, technical and organizational problems, large and small, according to a recent Dutch enquiry into the conditions necessary to make Schengen work.

To mind comes the privacy protection in relation to the concrete exchange of information, the execution of a manageable damage arrangement for border crossing police officers, the realizing of a network of communications, etc.

One of the more strategic questions posed when 'working' the actual Schengen Convention is the question of how this Convention can be executed via bilateral agreements and arrangements (in the border area). This question cannot, of course, be fully answered here. But, considering what has been accomplished in a number of border areas in the last few years, a 'principle of subsidiarity' could serve as a starting point. Whatever can be arranged via bilateral police cooperation in the border areas, should be so dealt with, what cannot be so organized that way, can eventually be completed via bilateral agreements. The advantage of this is that not only one can profit from the experiences gained in the past at the borders, but also that other arrangements are being created which may favourably involve the 'local' police services and their direct authorities as well as their national counterparts.

Finally, in the long run, arises the strategic question of how the mostly judicially orientated arrangement of the police cooperation in the Schengen Convention can and should be attuned to the evolution of the cross-border administrative cooperation arrangements. This problem was raised at the discussion of the latest developments in Nebedeag-Pol and at the start up of the police cooperation in the Antwerp-North Brabant border area. But, considering the Benelux Treaty concerning cross-border cooperation between territorial authorities of 1986, ratified, as the last one, by Belgium in 1990, this question will be put, sooner or later, in the whole of the Belgian-Dutch border area. Here again, easy solutions are not available. In order to prevent that this cooperation, in the long run, would deploy in various directions, it would be advisable to look for possibilities to create cross-border consulations between police, administrative and judicial authorities, either or not framed in Euro-regionally tinted cooperation agreements. It goes without saying that there is also still a lot of work here for the national judical and administrative authorities.

U.S. Police Activities in Europe

Ethan Nadelmann

I. Introduction

Look around Europe today and one finds well over one hundred U.S. law enforcement agents stationed in U.S. embassies and consulates and dozens of others here on temporary business. In Rome, to take a prominent example, the law enforcement group within the embassy includes representatives of the Drug Enforcement Administration (DEA), Federal Bureau of Investigation (FBI), Secret Service, Customs, Internal Revenue Service (IRS), Immigration and Naturalization Service (INS), Naval Investigative Service (NIS), Air Force Office of Special Investigations (AFOSI), Army Criminal Investigative Division (CID) and a former federal prosecutor representing the U.S. Attorney General. Meetings of the Italian-American Working Group on Organized Crime are periodically attended by the U.S. Attorney General and other top officials of U.S. law enforcement agencies. Italian officials in the Justice Ministry's Office of International Affairs work closely with their counterparts in the U.S. Justice Department's Office of International Affairs, processing requests for evidence, fugitives and the execution of letters rogatory. While the number of U.S. agencies represented in Rome is exceptional, the types and levels of law enforcement cooperation are not.

The international law enforcement presence of the U.S. government within and without Europe is unique in at least three respects. No other government maintains law enforcement representatives in so many foreign countries. No other government possesses such a multitude of law enforcement agencies, each with its own reasons for operating and locating abroad. And no other government has exercised such a powerful influence during this century on the criminal laws, procedures and investigatory tactics of other countries. Britain and France may have exercised a more profound influence on the criminal justice systems of the lands they colonized and ruled during their imperial conquests; and Napoleonic France and Nazi Germany may have succeeded in briefly maintaining supranational police forces more powerful than anything in evidence today; but the United States is certainly the first to establish a global police presence as well as the first to play such a major role in shaping the criminal justice norms of countries both within and beyond

Europe. There has, in short, been an Americanization of foreign criminal justice systems, the nature and implications of which I will elaborate upon below.

II. The Ambiguous Domain of International Criminal Law Enforcement

The extent and even the subject of U.S. law enforcement activities in Europe is not quite so clearly defined as one might think at first. The ambiguity stems first from the fact that U.S. police officials in Europe lack the very powers of arrest and other types of officially sanctioned coercion that define them as police agents within the United States. They serve as official representatives, engage in liaison activities, and engage in both passive and proactive criminal investigative activities – but their badges, subpoenas and warrants are backed by relatively little in the way of official coercive powers. The result is that they are obliged to operate not unlike private investigators, relying upon their investigative skills, personal and professional contacts and the reservoir of good will and professional courtesy that characterizes the contemporary transnational police subculture. Unlike private investigators, they can draw upon the diplomatic leverage of the U.S. ambassador when necessary. But also unlike private investigators, they are occasionally hampered by nationalistic sensitivities and even legal prohibitions that preclude certain types of investigative tactics by U.S. and other foreign police.

Two other sources of ambiguity concern the identity of police officials and the nature of their tasks. FBI and DEA agents stationed and otherwise present in Europe are officially employed by U.S. law enforcement agencies, identify themselves as U.S. police officials and engage in activities designed to advance the objectives of their agencies. But much of what they do may have relatively little to do with the enforcement of U.S. criminal laws. They may devote substantial time to diplomacy and public appearances; they may focus their energies on training local police officials; they may devote substantial effort to investigating violations of foreign laws that have little or nothing to do with U.S. laws or interests; and they may be called upon to employ their investigative skills in support of U.S. objectives, such as collection of political intelligence, unrelated to criminal law enforcement.

Conversely, many individuals other than U.S. law enforcement agents engage in activities directly related to the enforcement of U.S. criminal laws. U.S. consular officials have played an important role in

U.S. international criminal law enforcement activities since the nation's origins. Private detective agencies and assorted 'special agents' were frequently called upon to investigate the extraterritorial dimensions of U.S. criminal law violations during the latter decades of the nineteenth century, and they appear to be re-emerging as significant participants in international criminal law enforcement matters. Both U.S. law enforcement agencies and occasionally other agencies have hired and paid informants abroad for information on transnational criminal activities. The CIA and other U.S. intelligence agencies have long devoted personnel and other resources to investigating extraterritorial violations of U.S. laws – particularly those such as espionage, export control violations and weapons smuggling that implicate both criminal justice and national security interests. And U.S. military forces have been called upon in response to violations of U.S. laws, as when U.S. Air Force planes forced an Egyptian airliner carrying the hijackers of the Achille Lauro to land in Italy.

Yet another source of ambiguity involves the legality, illegality and extra-legality of international law enforcement actions as well as the extent to which criminal law violators are dealt with by criminal justice institutions. When police agents engage in illegal activities to apprehend criminals, we hesitate in classifying their actions as 'law enforcement.' The same is true when criminal activities, particularly state-sponsored terrorist acts, are met with military attacks and black-bag operations. Particularly ambiguous are counter-espionage activities, which lie at the legally murky nexus where the realms of criminal justice and national security interact. This is the most 'political' of international law enforcement domains. When the CIA and other U.S. intelligence agencies, including the counter-espionage section of the FBI, investigate espionage, they are in effect investigating violations of U.S. criminal laws even though their principal objectives often have little to do with prosecuting spies in American courts.

A final source of ambiguity involves the issues of extraterritoriality and jurisdiction. When U.S. law enforcers seek to extradite individuals who have committed murder within the United States and fled abroad, the issues are entirely straightforward. They become a little more complex when foreign governments, particularly in civil law nations, refuse to extradite citizens who have violated other governments' laws abroad and insist on trying them in their own courts instead. Both their reliance on nationality as a basis of jurisdiction and their practice of vicarious prosecution of offenders remain largely alien to U.S. notions of jurisdiction. More important for our purposes is whether offenses against U.S. citizens and interests abroad violate U.S. laws. Note that terrorist acts against U.S. citizens abroad did not violate U.S. law until Congress enacted legislation in 1984 specifically criminalizing such extraterritorial acts. Prior to 1984, U.S. law enforcement agencies often left the investigation of such offenses to foreign authorities, and whatever assistance they rendered had no impact on U.S. courts. The proliferation of federal statutes since the 1970s criminalizing extraterritorial offenses against U.S. interests and otherwise extending the reach of U.S. criminal laws to foreign countries explains much of the recent increase in U.S. international criminal law enforcement activities.

The ambiguities we encounter in trying to define the domain of international criminal law enforcement help remind us that law enforcement is in essence a 'political' activity, and that the underlying impetus of all international criminal law enforcement activities is the initial fact of criminalization by the state. It is important to recall that the origins of international law enforcement in Europe were intimately connected with the efforts of European governments to surveil and apprehend military deserters, vagabonds and political dissidents resident in other countries, and that many of the crimes for which they were sought no longer are regarded as criminal. Conversely, we do well to keep in mind that much of international law enforcement today is preoccupied with investigating and prosecuting activities that were not regarded as criminal a century ago. This is particularly true of transnational trafficking in heroin, cocaine, cannabis and other controlled psychoactive substances, as well as corollary activities such as money laundering that have been criminalized principally to supplement drug law enforcement efforts. But it is also true of insider trading and other violations of securities and commodities laws, new sorts of tax law violations and export controls, environmental depredations, trafficking in cultural artifacts, animals, ivory and other products of endangered animal species, and transnational migrations of people.

It is thus useful to distinguish among varying degrees of 'politicalness' in thinking about international criminal law enforcement. At one extreme are counter-espionage, counter-terrorism and export control activities. All of these implicate traditional notions of national security, invite the involvement of intelligence and military agencies, and provide substantial latitude for explicitly political and discretionary interventions into routine criminal justice processes. At the other extreme are extradition and other international law enforcement efforts directed at apprehending common murderers, rapists and thieves; these are typically handled primarily by criminal justice personnel with minimal political input by foreign ministry and diplomatic officials. In between lie a variety of activities that range from unilateral state efforts to enforce their own tax, customs and immigration laws to multilateral efforts to deter and investigate drug trafficking and other activities now criminalized by international conventions. The breadth and intensity of cooperation between U.S. and European law enforcement agencies today can be explained in good part by the fact that governments in Europe and North America see eye to eye politically on such a broad array of matters that most law enforcement issues have become non-contentious and effectively de-politicized.

The relationship between police and criminal laws is essentially a passive one. Criminal laws are created by legislatures and other law makers to protect the interests of the state and other powerful members of society; to deter, suppress and punish undesirable activities; to provide for order, security and justice among members of a community; and to give force and symbolic representation to the moral values, beliefs and prejudices of those who make the laws. Police and other law enforcement officials typically play a minor role in law creation, particularly in more open, democratic societies. Their role is essentially reactive, with them responding to criminalizations by governments and other political actions that generate new law enforcement tasks and responsibilities. The principal exceptions occur when law enforcement officials propose new criminalizations and criminal penalties designed to improve their capacity to deter and investigate more familiar crimes. These exceptions are most apparent today in the rapidly spreading network of criminalizations directed at activities linked to drug trafficking.

It is important, in analyzing U.S. police activities in Europe, to bear in mind two broader contexts. The first is the overall scope of U.S. international criminal law enforcement efforts, which include various prosecutorial endeavors, the work of offices specializing in international criminal law enforcement matters in the U.S. Justice Department, the Securities and Exchange Commission (SEC) and the State Department, the negotiation of extradition, mutual legal assistance and prisoner transfer treaties, the participation of high-level officials in the Justice Department and other departments, and the involvement of diplomatic personnel, intelligence agencies and the military. Police agencies are directly involved in most efforts to 'immobilize' transnational criminals by obtaining information, evidence and fugitives abroad. They provide most of the manpower, and perform most of the legwork, but their activities must be seen as part and parcel of overall U.S. international law enforcement efforts.

The second context is the global presence and efforts of U.S. police agents. Like most countries, the United States' most abundant and intensive international law enforcement efforts involve its neighbors. The

U.S. law enforcement relationship with Canada bears similarities with both U.S.-European and intra-European law enforcement relationships. The U.S.-Mexico law enforcement relationship bears less in common with European law enforcement relationships, although the crumbling of the Soviet bloc has begun to present central European governments, particularly Germany, with challenges increasingly similar to those the United States confronts along its southwest border. What most distinguishes the U.S. international police presence, however, is its scope and activism. Over 300 DEA agents are now stationed in approximately seventy cities in fifty countries; the military criminal investigative divisions maintain hundreds of agents outside the United States, the FBI and U.S. Customs claim dozens, and other U.S. agencies a handful. Although one can point to many similarities between DEA activities in Latin America and Asia and those in Europe – including the general challenges of operating in foreign territories and the specific challenges of trying to work in civil law countries – there is no European analogue to the DEA's Operation Snowcap in Bolivia and Colombia, with its paramilitary attacks on drug manufacturing labs. Important as the U.S. police presence in Europe is to both U.S. interests and European policing, its significance pales beside the import of U.S. law enforcement activities elsewhere.

III. The Evolution of U.S. Policing in Europe

The history of U.S. policing in Europe can be divided into various stages. The simplest is between the first 150 years, i.e. roughly the period before World War II, and the last fifty years, i.e. roughly the period since World War II. This division is, of course, characteristic of U.S. involvement in world affairs generally, reflecting as it does the United States' paramount power and leadership role in world politics following its triumph in the Second World War. Indeed, much of the impetus for the internationalization of U.S. criminal law enforcement emerged as part and parcel of this new global role. For our purposes, however, there is good reason to divide the pre and post-war eras each into three stages. The boundaries between each are somewhat hazy and overlapping, and I will generally ignore the exceptional but brief periods during which the United States was at war internally (1861-

1865) and externally (1917-1918 and 1941-1945), but certain distinctions are worth making.

III.1. The Pre-World War II Era

Between the United States' origins in 1789 and the end of the Civil War in 1865, U.S. police agents rarely had occasion to visit Europe. Apart from one short-lived extradition arrangement with Britain, no extradition treaties were negotiated until the 1840s. Consular and other diplomatic officials provided intelligence to domestic authorities on criminal matters such as slave trading, piracy and violations of U.S. customs laws. Most international law enforcement tasks were handled by naval forces and revenue cutters. Federal law enforcement agencies remained few and undeveloped. Customs agents ventured across the Canadian border and other land borders, but rarely further.[1] The two other federal police agencies – the Postal Investigative Service and the U.S. Marshals – had little need to look abroad. The one U.S. police official most engaged in international matters during this period was probably Jacob Hays, the High Constable of New York City, who exchanged frequent correspondence with European police officials.[2] The underdeveloped state of U.S. policing contrasted sharply with much of continental Europe, where policing had already attained a more professional and powerful degree of development.

The second stage extended from roughly the Civil War to World War I. Millions of Europeans immigrated to the United States and transatlantic commerce grew rapidly, both of which generated increasing demands for law enforcement cooperation with Europe. The spread of democracy and liberty in Europe also alleviated American reservations regarding cooperation in criminal matters. State Department officials negotiated dozens of extradition treaties. Municipal police departments in the United States created criminal investigative branches. Some, particularly the N.Y.P.D., began to interact with European agencies with regularity. Police chiefs and scholars began to study European police organization and investigative methods and familiarized themselves with developments in European police sciences, including the Bertillon and

1. United States Custom Service, *A History of Enforcement in the United States Customs Service, 1789-1875*, Washington: Department of the Treasury, 1986, 4-29, 30. The unnamed author of the report is Michael N. Ingrisano, Jr., former Acting Director, Information Services Division, United States Customs Service.
2. Astor, G., *The New York Cops; An Informal History*, New York: Charles Scribner's Sons, 1971, 14.

printing methods of criminal identification. The Secret Service was created in 1865 to investigate counterfeiting crimes. Its agents quickly emerged as the handymen of federal law enforcement, undertaking a great variety of tasks from investigation of smuggling to undercover espionage tasks during the 1898 war with Spain.[3] The Justice Department was created in 1870, and a Bureau of Investigation in 1908.[4] Most significantly, the Treasury Department began to station agents abroad. The first was one Frederick Augustus Starring, a graduate of Harvard and a major general in the Civil War, who served as special Treasury agent in Europe from 1869 to 1883.[5] By the turn of the century, Treasury agents were stationed in five European cities – Paris, London, Berlin, Cologne and St. Gall.[6] Also significant were the proliferation of multilateral conventions directed at the criminalization and suppression of the 'white slave traffic,' drug trafficking, pornography and counterfeiting – in all of which U.S. delegates played a role despite their Congressionally imposed exclusion from the League of Nations.

The handful of Americans most engaged in interactions with European police were a diverse lot: Thomas Byrnes, the police chief of New York City from 1880 to 1896 who assembled an extensive 'rogues' gallery of pictures of American and European criminals and corresponded regularly with European counterparts;[7] Joe Petrosino, head of the N.Y.P.D.'s Italian Squad who was murdered in Sicily in 1909 while gathering information on transnational mafiosi;[8] John Wilkie, chief of the Secret Service during the first decade of this century, who personally conducted investigations of counterfeiting and smuggling in Europe;[9] David Parker, chief special agent for the United States Post Office from 1876 to 1883, whose reputation was such that German postal authorities

3. See Dorman, M., *The Secret Service Story,* New York: Delacorte Press, 1967.
4. See Langeluttig, A., *The Department of Justice of the United States,* Baltimore, Maryland: The John Hopkins Press, 1927.
5. *History of Customs Enforcement,* 5:2.
6. Theobald, W.H., *Defrauding the Government,* New York: Myrtle Publishing Co., 1908, 353.
7. Reppetto, T.A., *The Blue Parade,* New York: Free Press, 1978, 52-68; and Byrnes, *T., Rogue's Gallery,* Secaucus, N.J.: Castle, 1988, first published by Chelsea House Publishers in 1887.
8. See Pitkin, T.M. and Cordasco, F., *The Black Hand; A Chapter in Ethnic Crime,* Totowa, N.J.: Littlefield, Adams & Co., 1977; Petacco, A., *Joe Petrosino,* New York: Macmillan Publishing Co., 1974, originally published in Italian by Mondadori Publishing Co., 1972; and Pozzetta, G.E., 'Another Look at the Petrosino Affair', *Italian Americana,* 1974, no. 1, 81-92.
9. Don Wilkie, as told to Luther, M.L., *American Secret Service Agent,* New York: Frederick A. Stokes Co., 1934, 16-27, 185-186.

turned to him for assistance in investigating theft of the mails;[10] and, most significantly, William Pinkerton, who succeeded his father, Allan, as chief of the Pinkerton Detective Agency and expanded the agency's clientele, offices and investigations throughout Europe and much of the rest of the world. So well known had the name 'Pinkerton' become by the 1890s that many Europeans thought it was the title of the American criminal police.[11]

During the third stage – the interwar period – U.S. federal police agencies increased their international activities while the international profiles of the big city police departments and the private detective agencies diminished in comparison. The most significant development was the rapidly growing number of Treasury agents stationed abroad. By 1937 (according to one report that I have not been able to confirm), forty-six Treasury agents were stationed throughout Europe.[12] The late 1930s also saw the first foreign postings by the Federal Bureau of Narcotics (FBN), which had been created in 1930 to better enforce drug prohibition laws. Particularly prominent in international police circles was Harry Anslinger, who had served as chief of the Prohibition Unit's Foreign Control Section during the late 1920s before being appointed the FBN's first director.[13] U.S. police agencies generally showed little interest in the Vienna-based International Criminal Police Commission (later known as Interpol). The N.Y.P.D. sent a delegate to the first meeting in 1923 and J. Edgar Hoover sent representatives during the late 1930s[14] – but Anslinger took the initiative in organizing a sort of 'mini-

10. Denniston, E., *America's Silent Investigators,* New York: Dodd, Mead & Co., 1964, 73-74.
11. Thorwald, J., *The Century of the Detective,* New York: Harcourt, Brace & World, 1965, 91. Also see Morn F., *'The Eye that Never Sleeps'; A History of the Pinkerton National Detective Agency*, Bloomington: Indiana University Press, 1982; Horan, J.D. and Swiggett, H., *The Pinkerton Story,* New York: G.P. Putnam's Sons, 1951, 161-200; and Horan, J.D., *The Pinkertons; The Detective Dynasty that Made History,* New York: Crown Publishers, 1967, 280-320.
12. Roark, G., *The Coin of Contraband,* Garden City, N.Y.: Doubleday & Co., 1964, 343.
13. See McWilliams, J.C., *The Protectors: Harry J. Anslinger and the Federal Bureau of Narcotics, 1930-1962,* Newark, Delaware: University of Delaware Press, 1989; Kinder, D.C. and Walker III, W.O., 'Stable Force in a Storm: Harry J. Anslinger and United States Narcotic Foreign Policy, 1930-1962', *Journal of American History,* 1986, 908-927; and three books co-authored by Anslinger, H. (with W. F. Tompkins), *The Traffic in Narcotics,* New York: Funk & Wagnalls, 1953; (with W. Oursler), *The Murderers,* New York: Farrar, Straus & Co., 1961; and (with J. D. Gregory), *The Protectors,* New York: Farrar, Straus & Co., 1964.
14. Meldal-Johnsen, T. and Young, V., *The Interpol Connection; An Inquiry into the International Criminal Police Organization,* New York: Dial Press, 1979, 41-51.

Interpol' of European and North American police officials to exchange information on transnational drug traffickers.[15]

The era before World War II is worth recalling for three reasons. It reminds us of the origins of international law enforcement and of the fact that much of what seems relatively new today in fact dates back decades and even centuries. It allows us to identify and examine patterns of change and continuity in the evolution of international law enforcement over a longer, and hence more revealing, time spectrum. And it obliges us to keep in mind the potential for the international criminal law enforcement agenda to change over time in ways that may be difficult to anticipate.

III.2. The Post-World War II Era

The dramatic internationalization of U.S. policing since the close of the Second World War was principally a consequence of two developments: the U.S. government's decision not to return to a policy of relative isolationism, as it had following the First World War, but rather to assume leading roles in the struggle against communism and the invigoration of the capitalist world; and the proliferation of transnational non-governmental activities – financial, industrial, legal, environmental and otherwise – in which the U.S. government perceived a political or regulatory interest.

Even absent this new internationalist perspective, however, two other developments would have obliged U.S. law enforcement officials to expand their international efforts. The more readily anticipated was the increase in transnational criminal activity that inevitably accompanied the dramatic growth in the volume of legitimate transnational intercourse. As transnational securities transactions, banking exchanges, commercial ventures and credit card charges all increased dramatically, so too did the number of frauds associated with them. One need only assume that the criminal proportion of overall transnational economic activity has remained constant to conclude that the overall magnitude of transnational criminal activity must have increased dramatically. Less readily anticipated, from the perspectives of the 1940s and 1950s, was the remarkable growth in the illicit traffic in cannabis, cocaine and heroin. Related to all these developments, moreover, was a persistent expansion in the reach of both the substantive criminal law and the claims of extraterritorial ju-

15. Block, A.A. and McWilliams, J.C., 'On the Origins of American Counterintelligence: Building a Clandestine Network', *Journal of Policy History*, 1989, 357.

risdiction to cover an ever broader array of undesirable activities. Much of this was driven, as before, by domestic politics. But much of it was also initiated and driven – to a far greater extent than ever before – by the advocacy efforts of federal law enforcement officials.

The United States' leadership role in the anti-communist struggle resulted in four significant developments in the domain of international law enforcement. First, police were needed to provide for law and order among the hundreds of thousands of U.S. military personnel stationed around the world, as well as between them and the host country populations. The criminal investigative dimension of this need was filled by the military investigative divisions, CID, NIS and AFOSI, each of which maintained hundreds of agents abroad. Second, a police training dimension was added to U.S. foreign assistance programs, motivated in part by the perceived need to bolster anti-communist governments and suppress communist insurgencies. These were targeted principally in Latin America and Asia, and supplemented by the similar efforts of European powers in their imperial and post-imperial territories. Third, U.S. law enforcement agencies were charged with investigating violations of new laws prohibiting the export of weapons and sophisticated technology to pro-Soviet and other unfriendly governments. And fourth, espionage activities directed against the United States needed to be investigated, not just by the intelligence agencies but – since criminal prosecution of spies is the principal counterespionage weapon employed by democratic governments – by law enforcement agents as well.

Apart from the national security incentives, the most important factor contributing to the internationalization of both crime and law enforcement was the growing ease of transnational interactions as a consequence of developments in technology. Increasingly rapid and accessible jet travel permitted both criminals and police to travel easily and quickly almost anywhere in the world. Advances in telecommunications allowed criminals to conspire and commit crimes transnationally even as the same advances facilitated transnational exchange of information and coordination of joint investigations among law enforcement agents. Computers with international hook-ups presented new opportunities for criminals, both in defrauding legitimate actors and in setting up their own operations; but they also provided police with more efficient means of keeping track of transnational criminals, exchanging intelligence with foreign counterparts, and creating data bases on criminals and criminal activities. In all these respects, crime and law enforcement have been internationalized by technological developments in much the same way as other types of international commerce and governmental regulation.

Almost as significant were the enactment of new laws that created new types of transnational crime. Some did so by criminalizing conduct that had not previously been criminalized. The Export Control Act of 1949 and subsequent legislation enhancing that act extended the reach of the criminal law to transnational activities that previously had been legal.[16] The crime of transnational money laundering did not exist until 1970 at the earliest, when Congress made it illegal to take $5,000 or more in or out of the country without reporting that fact, and it only attained independent standing in 1986, when Congress criminalized the act of money laundering.[17] By 1990, enforcement of criminal laws directed at money laundering had become a major preoccupation of U.S. international law enforcement efforts. Other laws extended the reach of U.S. criminal jurisdiction abroad, such as by criminalizing terrorist and other offenses and conspiracies against U.S. citizens and interests that previously had fallen outside the purview of American courts.

Many of these developments followed naturally from the nationalization of crime and crime control within the United States. The emergence of crime as a national issue, and of crime control as a federal responsibility, are best dated to 1964, when Senator Barry Goldwater focused attentions on rising crime rates during his presidential campaign and President Lyndon Johnson reluctantly responded by placing crime control on the federal agenda.[18] Both the nationalization of the crime issue and the federalization of crime control had received their first substantial impetuses during the 1930s, when the administration of Franklin Delano Roosevelt included crime control among the array of issues on his New Deal agenda.[19] Congressional interest in racketeering provided additional impetuses in following decades.[20] But by the 1960s, the inhibitions on federal intrusions into what had traditionally been perceived as domains of state jurisdiction had faded substantially. The Johnson administration laid the initial groundwork, after which the Nixon administration entered office committed to an aggressive federal involvement in

16. See Stenger, G., 'The Development of American Export Control Legislation After World War II', *Wisconsin International Law Journal*, 1987, 1-42.
17. See Nadelmann, E.A., 'Unlaundering Dirty Money Abroad: U.S. Foreign Policy and Financial Secrecy Jurisdictions', *Inter-American Law Review*, 1986, 33-82.
18. Caplan, G., 'Reflections on the Nationalization of Crime, 1964-1968', *Law and the Social Order* (Arizona State University Law Journal), 1973, 583-635.
19. See *Proceedings of the Attorney General's Conference on Crime Held December 10-13, 1934 in Memorial Continental Hall, Washington, D.C.* and the articles collected under the title 'Extending Federal Powers Over Crime' in *Law and Contemporary Problems*, 1934, 399-508.
20. See Bradley, C.M., 'Racketeering and the Federalization of Crime', *American Criminal Law Review*, 1984, 213-266.

crime control and a dramatic escalation in the 'war on drugs'.[21] The Ford and Carter administrations brought both a diminution in the rhetoric as well as revelations of legal and illegal excesses by federal police agencies. But the Reagan and Bush administrations revived the crime issue and sponsored dramatic increases in both the reach of federal criminal laws and the resources of federal criminal justice agencies. Despite modest reservations by its more liberal members, Congress endorsed most of these initiatives and occasionally supplemented them of its own accord.

The internationalization of crime and crime control represented extensions of these developments. Having declared a 'war on drugs', the Nixon administration focused substantial attentions and resources on the foreign sources of the heroin, cocaine and most of the marijuana consumed in the United States. Indeed, the international dimension was attractive both because it offered a rare domain of criminal justice activity where the federal government could predominate over state and local agencies and because it provided an inviting political target for those who preferred not to focus too much attention on the domestic causes for increasing illicit drug use. Similar motivations could be discerned in the international extensions of the anti-drug campaign during the 1980s. The rapid growth of the federal law enforcement agencies, in particular the BNDD and the DEA, also provided the institutional bases required to sustain a substantial international presence. As these agencies expanded their activities but found their investigations frustrated by both criminal ingenuity and restrictions on their investigative powers and capacities, they proposed and lobbied for new criminal legislation to improve their powers of detection and to increase the variety of legal stumbling blocks on which criminals and their accomplices might trip up. The results were laws requiring the divulsion of information about financial transactions, criminalizing involvement in the laundering of illicitly derived revenues, authorizing the forfeiture of assets associated with criminal activity, and otherwise seeking to complicate and uncover criminal endeavors.

For all of the U.S. law enforcement agencies, these developments have meant increases in interactions with foreign police, international travel, international investigations and, for many of the agencies, foreign offices. Some U.S. police agents – notably those of the DEA and the military's criminal investigative units – have become intimately involved in the more operational aspects of criminal investigation, typi-

21. Epstein, E.J., *Agency of Fear: Opiates and Political Power in America*, New York: G. P. Putnam's Sons, 1977.

cally in collaboration with foreign police officials. They have recruited and run informants, conducted physical and electronic surveillances, employed undercover operations, supervised controlled deliveries of illicit drugs and other illegal commodities, and so on. Many of the law enforcement agencies now station representatives overseas, and all are increasingly involved in developing and cultivating closer links with foreign counterparts. The internationalization of law enforcement, I should stress, has been very much a two-way street, even if most of the traffic still carry U.S. badges.

The first stage of the post-war era of international law enforcement extended until the late 1960s. Customs and FBN agents returned to their pre-war posts in Europe and elsewhere and created new offices. The FBI followed suit and posted a few dozen agents – referred to as legal attaches or LEGATs – to foreign posts with strict orders to refrain from the sorts of operational activities engaged in by FBN and Customs agents. The Secret Service opened an office in Paris with a few agents to keep an eye on counterfeiting operations in Europe. Treasury Department officials and FBN and Secret Service agents joined Interpol gatherings. J. Edgar Hoover, however, shunned the international agency, preferring to rely on his LEGAT network. The most active and operational U.S. police agents abroad were those employed by the military investigative branches. With ample budgets and few restrictions, they liaised informally with European and other police agencies, worked out of their own safe houses, employed informants, ran undercover operations and generally played an important role in raising European consciousness of American-style investigative methods. Their jurisdiction covered the entire spectrum of crimes from violent and larcenous conflicts between U.S. military personnel and local residents to espionage, export control violations, drug trafficking and frauds of every sort.

Apart from occupied countries such as West Germany, where U.S. occupation forces exercised a strong hand in the creation of post-war police forces, most European countries were relatively uninfluenced by the U.S. police presence. U.S. criminal justice officials no longer looked to Europe, as they had before the war, for models of police organization and innovations on criminal investigation. And most European criminal justice officials simply relied on the same organizational approaches and investigative techniques employed before the war – minus a few of the more proactive techniques that had been discredited by virtue of their association with fascist police forces. Interpol remained primarily a Euro-centric organization dominated by the French, with relatively little

U.S. involvement.[22] European police agencies discreetly accommodated the needs and tactics of the FBN and U.S. military investigators in their midst without resorting to any more fundamental changes in their laws and modi operandi.

The second stage of the post-war era extended from the late 1960s to the late 1970s. The principal development during this decade was the transformation of the U.S. federal drug enforcement agency – the BNDD from 1968 to 1973, and the DEA thereafter – into the first non-imperial, transnational police organization. In 1967, the last full year of FBN's existence, the budget of the Treasury Department's drug agency was approximately three million dollars. Roughly a dozen of its three hundred agents were stationed in eight locations outside the United States. Six years and two bureaucratic reorganizations later, in the last full year of BNDD operations, the drug agency boasted a budget of $74 million and 1446 total agents, of whom 124 were abroad in 47 offices in 33 countries. By 1976, just before a minor contraction in its size, the DEA's budget was just short of $200 million; 228 of its 2117 agents were stationed overseas, in 68 offices in 43 countries. In less than a decade, a small overseas complement of American drug enforcement agents had grown into the first global law enforcement agency with operational capabilities. By contrast, the overseas presence of the FBI, U.S. Customs, the Secret Service and the military investigative branches during this same period either contracted or increased only slightly.

The principal impetus for this development was President Nixon's 'declaration of war' against transnational drug trafficking. The international law enforcement dimension of his campaign included not just the proliferation of U.S. drug enforcement agents abroad but also greater attentions and efforts by the CIA, the State Department and U.S. embassies around the world.[23] The stated objectives focused on reducing the flow of illicit drugs to the United States and 'immobilizing' transnational drug traffickers. Substantial efforts were also devoted, however, to expanding and consolidating the global drug prohibition regime. New international drug conventions were negotiated, foreign governments were lobbied and pressured to change their drug laws, and foreign criminal justice officials were encouraged to work closely with U.S. international drug enforcement efforts.

The consequences of the American campaign in Europe were modest compared to those elsewhere, but nonetheless significant. Unlike the

22. Anderson, M., *Policing the World: Interpol and the Politics of International Police Co-operation*, New York: Oxford University Press, 1989.
23. Epstein, E.J., *op.cit.*

U.S. Public Safety program, which provided police training to thousands of police officials in less developed nations, the U.S. international drug enforcement effort opened its training programs to European and other police officials from more developed nations. By the 1980s, a substantial proportion of European police officials specializing in drug enforcement had enrolled in BNDD/DEA training courses, had opportunities to work closely with U.S. drug enforcement agents, and had generally been exposed to American attitudes and norms regarding the investigation of drug trafficking. In some countries, such as Belgium and Austria, U.S. drug enforcement agents exercised a profound influence on the organization and tactics of new drug enforcement units. In Germany, many of the state-level criminal investigative units (the Landeskriminalamt) as well as the increasingly powerful federal police agency (the Bundeskriminalamt) looked to the DEA and, to a lesser extent, the FBI, for models and guidance. And even in the Netherlands, Italy, Spain and elsewhere, local drug enforcement units inevitably were influenced by the DEA's activities, programs and outlook.

The third stage of the post-war era began in the late 1970s and continues today. Three features stand out. The first is the consolidation and institutionalization of American influences on European drug enforcement specifically and criminal investigation more generally. By the late 1980s, most European police agencies claimed specialized drug enforcement units and most had begun stationing police liaisons in foreign cities both within Europe and beyond. More significantly, many U.S.-style investigative techniques once shunned in much of Europe – including undercover operations, controlled deliveries, the practice of 'flipping' informants, and sizeable payments to informants – had been widely adopted and formally sanctioned by European courts and legislatures. It is, I believe, accurate to speak of an 'Americanization' of European drug enforcement even as we acknowledge the powerful influence of intra-European forces and developments in policing. The DEA has largely succeeded in attaining its broader objectives: the creation of effective vicarious drug enforcement capabilities in Europe, the institutionalization of transgovernmental links with European drug enforcement units, and the widespread adoption of its own investigative and professional norms in Europe.

The second feature is the expansion of other U.S. police activities in Europe – exemplified by the depiction of the U.S. law enforcement presence in Rome with which I began this article. During the 1980s, U.S. Customs reversed the contraction in its overseas presence of the previous decade and began opening and re-opening offices abroad. Its agents focused primarily on investigating violations of U.S. money laundering and export control laws, but additional efforts were devoted to improving transgovernmental cooperation among customs officials in a wide array of customs matters. The FBI also increased its presence and activities abroad as it was called upon to extend its investigations of organized crime to Italy and elsewhere in Europe and as new federal statutes criminalizing terrorist offenses against U.S. citizens and interests abroad provided a new basis of extraterritorial jurisdiction. More significant than the modest increase in the FBI's network of LEGATs was the dramatic increase in FBI agent travels and interactions abroad, including intensive involvement in major transnational criminal investigations such as the 'Pizza Connection' case and the terrorist explosion of Pan Am Flight 103 over Lockerbie, Scotland.[24] The Secret Service opened new offices in Europe and participated actively in efforts to develop a network of counter-counterfeiting specialists throughout Europe. Other federal law enforcement agencies such as INS, IRS and the Bureau of Alcohol, Tobacco and Firearms expanded their transnational ties. The Justice Department initiated a policy of stationing U.S. attorneys abroad. And U.S. involvement in Interpol increased dramatically, with DEA and FBI agents stepping into important positions at Interpol headquarters, a dynamic chief of the U.S. national central bureau, Richard Stiener, playing an important role in the politics and policy making of the organization, and a U.S. police official, John Simpson, serving a term as Interpol's president.[25]

The third feature is the proliferation of U.S. law enforcement activities, treaties and linkages over and above the police level. In 1979, the Justice Department created an Office of International Affairs (OIA) within its Criminal Division and the State Department created an Office of Law Enforcement and Intelligence (L/LEI) in its Legal Adviser's Office. By 1990, the number of attorneys in OIA had increased tenfold from the four present at its inception. During the mid-1980s, the Securities and Exchange Commission followed suit and created its own office of international law enforcement. Attorneys in OIA and L/LEI negotiated mutual legal assistance treaties (MLATS) – first with Switzerland and thereafter with Turkey, the Netherlands, Italy and Belgium as well as other governments outside Europe – and pursued negotiations with many others, including (most frustratingly) Germany. Extradition

24. See Blumenthal, R., *Last Days of the Sicilians,* New York: Times Books, 1988; Sterling, C., *Octopus: The Long Reach of the International Sicilian Mafia,* New York: W. W. Norton & Co., 1990; and Emerson, S. and Duffy B., *The Fall of Pan Am 103; Inside the Lockerbee Investigation,* New York: G. P. Putnam's Sons, 1990.
25. See Anderson, M., *op.cit.*

treaties were renegotiated to cover more offenses, narrow the 'political offense' exception and otherwise reduce pre-existing obstacles to efficient extradition processes. Rather than negotiate bilateral prisoner transfer treaties with each European government, the U.S. government simply ratified the European Convention on the Transfer of Sentenced Persons.[26]

The most contentious dimension of U.S. law enforcement activities in Europe during the 1980s involved U.S. assertions of extraterritorial jurisdiction in violation of European secrecy and blocking statutes. These arose most frequently when U.S. prosecutors sought and obtained federal judicial support for their efforts to oblige European banks and other companies to hand over financial and corporate documents. Their tactics, known as '*Bank of Nova Scotia* subpoenas' and '*Ghidoni* waivers,' aroused substantial ire among European bankers and government officials – but also proved successful both in obtaining evidence in individual cases and in pressuring European governments to change their laws and negotiate treaties desired by U.S. law enforcement authorities. U.S. influences could readily be found behind the wave of legislation throughout Europe criminalizing money laundering and insider trading and instituting asset forfeiture laws. By the late 1980s, criminal law enforcement matters ranging from drug trafficking to terrorism and environmental offenses could also be found on the agendas of the G-7 meetings of presidents and prime ministers.

IV. The Future of U.S. Policing in Europe

Certain trends in the evolution of U.S. policing in Europe appear likely to continue in predictable directions. The 1990s will likely see the further 'Americanization' of European drug enforcement as DEA-style investigative methods are institutionalized in more and more countries. Relations between U.S. and European police agencies will become even more intimate as formal relationships proliferate and informal ties deepen. European concerns regarding the spread of organized crime will lead to new imports of U.S. criminal laws, policies and investigative methods. Intelligence and counter-intelligence agencies in search of new missions will focus increasing efforts on transnational criminality, one consequence of which will be intensified turf conflicts and the emergence of new legal issues in international criminal law enforcement.

26. TIAS 10824.

And the domain of international criminal law enforcement will include a growing number of criminal matters, many of which will be handled on an informal, transgovernmental and essentially apolitical basis.

The principal challenges confronting U.S. police agencies in Europe will probably be threefold. They will, first of all, be obliged to respond to the rapid Europeanization and (in Cyrille Fijnaut's words) 'Communitization' of policing in Europe.[27] Most of the developments associated with these processes are viewed favorably by U.S. law enforcement officials insofar as they promise a more homogeneous and increasingly effective law enforcement partner in Europe. But the same processes will also involve some displacement of U.S. law enforcement influences in Europe as well as the need to work out evolving relationships with intra-European police organizations such as the nascent Europol. Although European law enforcement interests and perspectives are unlikely to diverge from those of the United States in any substantial way during the 1990s, the differences that do emerge will no longer be so malleable by the United States.

The second challenge has already begun with the dissolution of the Soviet Union and the opening of Eastern Europe. The implications for the United States are relatively minor compared to those for Western Europe, but U.S. law enforcement officials have little choice but to work out new relationships with Eastern Europe and the successor states to the Soviet Union and Yugoslavia. Smugglers of illicit drugs and other commodities are already working in and through many of these countries. U.S. law enforcement officials have begun to establish working relationships and to provide assistance. U.S. Customs had a substantial headstart in this regard, having developed professional relations with Customs officials in Eastern Europe even before the collapse of the socialist dictatorships. But the DEA and the FBI find themselves venturing into relatively new territory as they start collaborating with Eastern European police officials and stationing liaisons in their major cities. Many of these countries are likely to prove hospitable havens for transnational criminals during the 1990s. Local police forces are not equipped to deal with the challenges of transnational crime in newly open societies. Resources for criminal justice will likely be limited. And impoverished governments eager to attract and retain hard currency will probably not be vigilant in expelling illicit enterprises, identifying and turning away 'dirty money,' and dealing with local corruption.

27. Fijnaut C., 'The "Communitization" of Police Cooperation in Western Europe', in: Schermers, H.G. et al., *Free Movement of Persons in Europe,* Dordrecht: Martinus Nijhoff Publishers, 1993, 75-92.

The third challenge cannot be identified with any certainty. It involves the emergence of new and perhaps unanticipated types of transnational criminality. Drug trafficking has dominated U.S. international criminal law enforcement concerns for over two decades and will probably continue to exercise a major influence during the 1990s and beyond. U.S. drug enforcement efforts in Europe have always focused on heroin, with modest but increasing attentions devoted to cocaine. This may change as relatively new drugs become popular on both sides of the Atlantic. One potential candidate is MDMA, the synthetic drug known as Ecstasy. But it also possible that transnational drug trafficking may diminish as a significant transatlantic law enforcement concern if illicit drug consumption drops substantially or shifts toward substances produced domestically. Police may find more of their efforts focusing on environmental offenses and trafficking in counterfeit products, armaments, nuclear materials and other dangerous items. New terrorist groups may emerge. The future agenda of U.S. international police efforts is, in short, impossible to predict with any certainty.

Laudatio on Behalf of the Jury on the Occasion of the Presentation of the First SMP Publication Prize on 22nd October 1992

Cyrille Fijnaut

Ladies and Gentlemen,

Now that the Vice-President of the Dutch Police and Society Foundation, Mr H. Wiegel, has briefly sketched the reasons behind our Foundation's decision some years ago to institute the prize which he will shortly be presenting to Dr W. Bruggeman, I would like to tell you – on behalf of the Jury and with the endorsement of the Preparatory Committee – why the first presentation of this prize is being made to the author of the substantial dissertation: *Naar een vernieuwde statistiek voor de reguliere politiediensten in België* (Towards More Modern Statistics for the Regular Police Forces of Belgium), Brussels, Politeia, 1992. But before I go any further, since this is the first award, I would like to tell you something of the way in which the Jury and the Preparatory Committee set to work. I don't intend to bore you with procedures. I don't simply want to underline how much has been done and how hard everyone has had to work on and off for the past two years. But I do want to give you the opportunity to judge the quality of the Jury's ultimate assessment for yourself. Just to make it clear, the Jury consisted of the following persons, besides myself: S. Boekman LLB (member of the Dutch Supreme Court), Prof. A.C. 't Hart LLB (State University of Leiden), E. Nordholt BA (Commissioner of Police, Amsterdam), H.D. Tjeenk Willink LLB (Chairman of Dutch Parliament's Upper House), with P.J.P.M. van Lochem BA, LLB (Executive Director, Fire Brigade Academy) as secretary.

The statutes of the Publication Prize are not very specific as to the assessment and selection procedure. Clause 1.4. indicates that the initial selection of works is the responsibility of a Preparatory Committee and Clause 3.4. informs us that the Jury's task is to assess the value of the police studies put forward by the Preparatory Committee. Clause 4.5. stipulates that the Preparatory Committee is to apply the same assessment criteria as the Jury, the latter being responsible for drawing up these criteria. And that is all! Just over two years ago we were given the assignment of interpreting these very general indications as to the methodology of the Jury and the Preparatory Committee and determining the boundaries. The members of both bodies met in The Hague in November 1990 to that end. Leaving aside the discussions on how the institution of the Publication Prize was to be made public as early as possible – the results of these discussions are well known to all of you, thanks to the commendable efforts of the publisher Gouda Quint: the conspicuous posters, exhibited all over the Netherlands and even, on a more selective basis, abroad –, the meeting was primarily concerned with the criteria to be applied in the award of this prize. These discussions led to the drawing up of initial 'guidelines' for the Preparatory Committee: beneficial to both society and police; the quality of the analysis, recognizable for instance from the penetrative level of the definition of the problem and the consistency of the argumentation; an original publication was preferable, one which – probably from an unexpected viewpoint – took a critical stand with regard to established values or schools of thought; subject relevance, if possible practical relevance, which is at least recognizable within policing in the broadest sense; the outward appearance of the produced work, not least in stylistic terms; conformation to a certain international standard: 'no reward for dwarves (and I quote almost literally) if there are giants around'.

These then are the initial criteria with which the Preparatory Committee began on its inventory of publications – publications in Dutch and also, as Clause 2.2. of the Statutes mentions, publications in other languages and, therefore, also foreign publications which might provide a contribution to police studies in the Netherlands and which appeared or were published in the two calendar years preceding the presentation of the award (in accordance with Clause 2.3. of the Statutes). The final report of the chairman of the Preparatory Committee – Mr P.J.P.M. van Lochem, who was also secretary of the Jury -- indicates that the Committee met a total of five times. I would like, here and now, to offer a vote of thanks to Mr Van Lochem on behalf of the Jury for all the correspondence he dealt with and the many organizational tasks he undertook in his double capacity. In the course of its discussions, the Committee supplemented, honed and classified the criteria which were originally drawn up in consultation with the Jury. The Committee especially emphasized the importance of the social relevance which the prize-winning entry should have in terms of the gravity of the problem being dealt with, in social, political or humanitarian terms, the size of the group which would find the publication relevant and the accessibility of the work for parties that might be interested. Secondly, in the course of 1991-1992, the members of the Committee tried – and not without success, fortunatel – to apply the refined criteria systematically to publications which they themselves had discovered or which had been submitted to the Jury. There were eleven such submissions, eight of them from abroad, which was not a bad start. And when I tell you that the original list comprised some 150 Dutch language works, I am sure you will agree that besides Mr van Lochem the other members of the Committee – Dr F.A.C.M. Denkers, Prof.Dr J. Naeyé, Messrs A.B. Hoogenboom and A.J. Kuijvenhoven – also deserve a warm round of applause for all their efforts.

After the initial selection – on the basis of the criteria mentioned above – the Committee was left with 25 Dutch language and a few foreign publications in other languages. All these publications were then subjected to reassessment by the Committee and the Chairman of the Jury, this second reading being far more thorough, of course. As had already been agreed, the purpose of this reassessment was to come to a final selection of six publications which would be submitted to the Jury. Of the six publications which found their way through to the final round, four were from the Netherlands and two from foreign authors. The remarkable point about this decision was the great unanimity of the members of the Preparatory Committee with regard to the order in which at least five of the publications involved should be eligible for the prize; there was evidently some difference of opinion with regard to one contender.

At an early stage the Jury and the Preparatory Committee had agreed that details of the six publications which were nominated, as it were, would not be made public. I shall, of course, abide by that agreement ... mainly, at least. I have the express permission of the Jury to tell you of one publication which was and still is highly spoken of by many members of the Preparatory Committee, and that is the book by Prof.Dr R. Reiner: *Chief Constables: Bobbies, Bosses or Bureaucrats* (Oxford, Oxford University Press, 1991). The review of this book by A.B. Hoogenboom and A. Cachet in the *Tijdschrift voor de Politie* (Magazine for the Police) – which magazine also deserves a special word of thanks for its extensive coverage of activities around the Publication Prize – indicates that the book is not only well-written and readable but also one which, at least as far as subject matter goes, is innovative and certainly relevant to us here in the Netherlands from a social viewpoint, taking our plans for a rigorous transformation of policing in the direction of the British model into account. But what one critic suggested, reading between the lines, is true: that relevance is not obvious from a first glance. To make it more obvious, Jury member Mr E. Nordholt and the other 25 new-style chiefs of police should really be cross-examined in the same way and about the same subjects as Prof. Reiner's 40 or more chief constables, but then within the Dutch context.

And here I come to the hard core of my commendation: praise for Dr W. Bruggeman for his study. As everyone knows, Belgian dissertations, even in the field of policing, are generally fairly bulky: they not only have to demonstrate the ability of the author to carry out scientific research on his own account, they also have to demonstrate that the author has a thorough understanding of the specific subject in question. Dr W. Bruggeman's dissertation is – and I am tempted to add: fortunately! – no exception to this rule. 700 or so pages of text, well larded with footnotes and supplemented with dozens of pages full of biblio-graphical references, leave us in no doubt as to the competence of the author in this field: criminal statistics in general and policing statistics in particular. And I can only refer anyone who thinks that such a study is unreadable by definition – and I cannot be entirely sure that no such person is to be found in the ranks of the Dutch police – to the words of one of the members of the Jury who had never previously read anything on this subject: 'I must admit that I picked up Bruggeman's book in trepidation, but was almost immediately caught up in his arguments and soon found myself completely engrossed if not entranced'. It is, then, my honour to explain how that choice was made, on the basis of the criteria which were formulated for the assessment of the various publications.

In the first place I can mention the originality of the publication. This is demonstrated not only by the fact that it is one of the very few European studies on this particular subject, discounting a few somewhat older German and English publications, but also by the fact that it offers a lucid link between developments in the theory of and research into criminality on the one hand and such a practical, if not prosaic, subject as policing statistics on the other hand. Beside this, both the methodology behind the study and the approach are certainly original: as far as we have been able to ascertain, as extensive and thorough a comparative study has never before been undertaken; developments and discussions in many Western countries are included, in a very orderly manner of course. At this moment, Dr Bruggeman's work is undoubtedly the primary source of information with regard to background, development and application of policing statistics in this corner of the world. And what applies in general certainly applies in particular: never before has the situation in Belgium been analyzed so precisely in literature. That is almost self-evident.

The originality of the study also means – and that was a criterion – that many concepts about the intrinsic value and practical usefulness of policing statistics are put to test and ultimately consigned to the academic scrap heap. The winning work can, in that sense, certainly be classed as critical, and self-critical too (the latter classification occurring far less frequently in the academic world than the former), since the police, including the Belgian state police force (Rijkswacht) up to and even including the executives of the general staff of the state police who work under the guidance of the author himself, are not spared an academic caning. To be honest, the study leaves very little of the current state of affairs in the field of policing statistics intact. But the fascinating thing is, that the very demolition of current ideas and practices – which the author accomplishes with a courteous flourish – lays the foundations for a more worthwhile, more practicable construction, or even reconstruction. Unfortunately, this process of demolition and reconstruction is given insufficient attention in the formal conclusions of the work. Anyone scanning through the work might be prompted to ask: 'do these conclusions really merit 700 pages full of text?' That the conclusions fail to offer a ready-made recipe for adequate policing statistics is another matter for regret, but on the other hand perhaps such a practical result is perhaps too much to expect from a dissertation.

The appeal of this study lies not only in the dynamics of the thought processes of its author. It also has to do with the subject: policing statistics, and that which lies behind it, i.e. criminality, not only as objective data but also as subjective fact. And that is a subject which, in the words of colleague J. van Weringh, perpetually occupies and concerns us, today far more so than ten, twenty or thirty years ago. Dr Bruggeman does not belittle that fact, but he shows us how intangible it is, even in policing statistics which usually provide good, if not the best, pointers for at least part of the problem. But, fortunately – as I say – he does not leave it at that. He goes on to give a detailed sketch of the conditions which should be fulfilled by statistics in order for them to really say something. And it is especially the way in which Dr Bruggeman does this, with the help of in-depth examination of problem elements and by alluding to general social developments, that captures and keeps the attention of the reader. In other words, his book is lively, full of action, even though it bears traces of the Prussian style staccato that characterizes so much of the Rijkswacht's prose. In the same breath I would like to add that a little more editorial attention would certainly have benefited the manuscript.

By way of the originality and the attractiveness of this work I arrive at its relevance, and especially its relevance for the police forces of the Netherlands. Let me put it this way: its relevance in social and policing terms is not the point. All the questions which this dissertation raises touch on the major domestic policing problems which face us in this day and age – not only in parliament and within the legal system but also at the core of our society, particularly in the much older inner city areas. Relevant, too, is the way the author deals with these problems and the general procedure he sketches for their solution. Even if only because his method counsels caution and restraint, especially in politics, in the application of the police and the judiciary for these solutions. But also because his own well-considered, thorough approach might offer a remedy for the ease, or dare I say, nonchalance with which even in the police force itself 'criminal things' are alleged and done. Not without reason did one of the members of the Jury remark, after reading the book, that the author had made some 'very wise comments' in the book.

If I focus the point about relevance on policing in the Netherlands, then I can – indeed must – be brief. We have had national so-called policing statistics for a long time. Almost 150 years if we take the concept loosely, almost 100 years if we take a narrower definition. In all that time there have not been very many changes. And that very continuity has its advantages, as we can learn from recent CBS research (Dutch Central Statistical Office) into the developments in criminality as registered by the police in the period from 1950 to 1990. But Dr Bruggeman's investigations confront us with the other side of the coin: in terms of design and content they are hopelessly out of date, both in the light of developments in criminology and with a view to the transformation of the Dutch police service into a single, though territorially and functionally segmented, force. This force will be committed to carrying out national policies which are based on an analysis of problems and which are modified on the basis of analysis of cause and effect. As far as the efforts of the Dutch police are concerned and their endeavours to improve their service at a local level over the last few years by means of a statistical analysis of criminality problems, I can only say that these have been very innovative, also when viewed in an international perspective. But anyone who takes the trouble to study the various statistical exercises which are carried out here and there, not only in the big cities but elsewhere too, on the basis of Dr Bruggeman's dissertation, will soon come to the conclusion that not only in Belgium but in the Netherlands, too, there is much room for improvement. The relevance of the dissertation for the Dutch police firm – an unpleasant word which also arose in the course of the discussions on criteria – is therefore indisputable.

Ladies and Gentlemen,

With these words I have fulfilled my obligations as chairman of the Jury. With words of commendation I have set out for you the reasons why the publication *Towards More Modern Statistics for the Regular Police Forces of Belgium* has been awarded the first Publication Prize of the Dutch Police and Society Foundation. On a personal note I would like to add that I was particularly pleased that this Dutch award is going to a Belgian, a Flemish, study especially since it was written by a man who, in recent years, has as no other tried to forge a link between the police forces on either side of the border in the Dutch speaking area. Nomen est omen.

Prof. Dr C. Fijnaut, Chairman of the Jury

www.ingramcontent.com/pod-product-compliance
Lightning Source LLC
LaVergne TN
LVHW102227300926
849160LV00005B/60
* 9 7 8 9 0 6 5 4 4 7 2 1 0 *